BYE-GONES

Bye-gones

**Collected from old volumes of folklore
by
RICHARD HOLLAND**

Gwasg Carreg Gwalch

ISBN: 0-86381-239-2

Cover design:
"What help are glasses and torchlights
in your alchemical search, if you are not
enlightened from within."

First published in 1992 by Gwasg Carreg Gwalch,
Capel Garmon, Llanrwst, Gwynedd, Wales.

☎ 0690 710261

Printed in Wales

MRS HARDCASTLE: *Ay, your times were fine times indeed . . . I hate such old-fashioned trumpery.*

MR HARDCASTLE: *And I love it. I love everything that's old: old friends, old times, old manners, old books, old wine.*

CONTENTS

Bye-Gones — Preface

From 1871 to 1939, with two brief interruptions, including one during the First World War, *The Oswestry Advertizer* newspaper published two columns, *Bye-Gones* and *In Field, Lane and Garden*. Every two months these columns, under the general heading of *Bye-Gones*, were bound up to form a periodical distinct from the newspaper, and every two years these periodicals were further bound up to form library volumes with a limited print-run of 200. It is from the collection of these volumes held by Clwyd County Library Headquarters in Mold that I have taken the forthcoming extracts.

Bye-Gones was a forum for those interested in the history and rural life of Wales and the Border Counties. A Queries section published requests for information on particular subjects by amateur historians and naturalists and a Replies section published answers and suggestions from their fellow readers. What makes *Bye-Gones* an exciting reference for today's historians is that the individual nature of the contributions makes much of the information contained within it unique: personal experiences of natural or supernatural phenomena, or retellings of localised folklore, for example.

These individual offerings were supplemented by extracts with relevance to Wales and the Marches from other papers and periodicals, including the popular, London-based *Notes and Queries* and regular English translations of the Welsh periodical *Cymru Fu*. In addition there was a newsy section compiled by the editors, called Current Notes.

Contained within this present volume you will find some of the best of *Bye-Gones*, including some fascinating folklore and archaic customs; ghost and UFO sightings and the survival of witchcraft; oddities of nature; bizarre coincidences; the experiences of great historical and literary figures in the Principality; some extraordinary local characters; and a whole host of other historical snippets pertaining to Wales and its Border Counties.

In editing these extracts I have sought to retain the original style of the narrative — including some shocking spellings of place-names! — while trimming out repetetive "in answer to . . . " or "I would be grateful for information on" phrases. The extracts have been dated and fully credited (although usually initials only or pseudonyms were given). Those supplied by the editor have been credited to "Ed".

My thanks to the ever-helpful staff of Clwyd County Library HQ in Mold for allowing me to borrow their precious *Bye-Gones* volumes and to the library of the University College of North Wales in Bangor for help in working out *Bye-Gones'* chronology.

Happy delving!

Pennant's Drunken Revels

THOMAS PENNANT — Of this distinguished Tourist Dr Johnson said, "Pennant is the best traveller I have ever read; he observes more things than anyone else does." In 'Walpoliana', No.169, Vol 1, we have this account of him:

"Mr Pennant is a most ingenious and pleasing writer. His Tours display a great variety of knowledge, expressed in an engaging way. In private life I am told he has some peculiarities and even eccentricities. Among the latter may be classed his singular antipathy to a wig — which, however, he can suppress, till reason yields a little to wine. But when this is the case, off goes the wig next to him and into the fire!

"Dining once at Chester with an officer who wore a wig, Mr Pennant became half seas over; and another friend that was in company carefully placed himself between Pennant and wig, to prevent mischief. After much patience, and many a wistful look, Pennant started up, siezed the wig, and threw it into the fire. It was in flames in a moment, and so was the officer, who ran to his sword. Down stairs runs Pennant and the officer after him, through all the streets of Chester. But Pennant escaped, from superior knowledge of topography. A wag called this "Pennant's Tour in Chester".

January 14, 1874   *Eliola*

The Dreadful Vicar of Llanidloes

The following petition from the 'Calendar of State Papers Domestic' 1637 (p.531) may interest your readers.

J. Arthur Price

"Nov. 10. Petition of Owen Gwyn to Archbishop Laud.

John Roberts, Vicar of Llanidloes, co. Montgomery, stands guilty of divers misdemeanours of ecclesiastical cognisance, and amongst others for repelling his parishioners from Holy Communion, not using the form of burial of the dead, profaning the altar by receiving money thereon, casting the surplice and Communion book on the floor, railing, quarreling and striking in the Church porch, breaking down ancient pews and tombstones, christening children by other names than the godfathers gave, denying his own father and turning him out to seek his lodging, cutting the surplice into pieces and using them for towels, permitting

persons with muskets to shoot at pigeons within the Church, and speaking against declaration for lawful recreations on Sundays. Prays that upon articles and bond a warrant may be granted for Roberts to answer."
October 6, 1897

A Leeky Theory

I am not familiar with the "ridiculous legend of the English" concerning the origin of the wearing of the leek, which I find in 'Cambrian Superstitions' by W. Howells (Tipton, 1831) —

"The Welsh in olden days were so much infested by Ourang Outangs that they could obtain no peace day or night, and, being powerless to extirpate them, invited the assistance of the English, who responded, but in mistake killed the men and the monsters. And so it came to pass that, to prevent the repetition of so lamentable an error, and to distinguish the human inhabitants from the Ourang Outangs, the English decreed the Welsh to wear a Leek in their hats."
September 6, 1899   *W.O.*

A Second Leeky Theory

Mr P. Llewellyn, in some notes to a poem of his at the commencement of the present century, says that he has been confidently assured that the leek is not the original emblem of Wales, but the sive or chive, which is common to every peasant's garden. The sive partakes of the smell and taste of the onion and leek, but is not so unfragrant as, and is much prettier than, the latter. It grows in a wild state on the banks of the Wye, much larger than when planted in gardens. According to Mr Llewellyn the manner in which the sive became the Welsh national emblem was as follows:

"As a Prince of Wales was returning victorious from battle, he wished to have some leaf or flower to commemorate the event; but it being winter, no plant or shrub was seen until they came to the Wye, when they beheld the sive, which the Prince commanded to be worn as a memorial of the victory."
April 15, 1885   *Verax*

11

John Milton A Welshman

The silly season, being delayed this year by the press of parliamentary business, has set in with more than its usual severity. The first crop of the *Western Mail* is a 'Remarkable Geneological Discovery' from which we extract the following:

"In the year 1605 there lived in the parish of Glan-pwll-y-domen, Montgomeryshire, a blacksmith, Shon ap Shenkin by name, who was as celebrated for the quality of his voice as for his skilled workmanship. His fame penetrated to the remotest corners of Wales, whence farmers brought their ploughshares and reaping hooks to be repaired and sharpened, while their wives and daughters accompanied them, attracted by the hope of hearing the harmonious blacksmith warble out some melodious notes.

"I pass over sundry incidents of a romantic nature which are not essential to this narrative, and come to the year 1607, when our hero was induced to compete for admission to the sacred circle of the Bards of Britain, in which he was not only completely successful, but the assembled bards were so struck by the number and variety of his songs, that they unanimously dubbed him Mil Tôn, and was thereafter known to his contemporaries as Shon Mil Tôn, or John of the Thousand Songs.

"Soon after this Shon got married to a lassie from Cardiganshire, and settled down in his native village, where, in the year following, his eldest son, afterwards the great poet, was born. A few years after this event, troublous times befel the country, when men began turning their ploughshares into swords, and seeing a chance at bettering himself at this, Shon migrated to London, where he eventually set up the sign of the Spread Eagle in Broad-street. His name Shon Mil Tôn was anglicised to John Milton, which name his son was destined to immortalize."

September 29, 1880   *Ed.*

Match Seller's Song

Previously to the general use of lucifer matches, every household kept a "tinder box", containing a small compartment for tinder, and another for flints, steel and brimstone matches. The best tinder was made by burning a piece of old linen, cotton was not so good. It was burnt quickly and the flame quickly extinguished by pressure into the box. The matches were very thin narrow chips of dry fir wood or stiff shavings, and pointed, and tipped with brimstone at each end.

The flintstones and matches were hawked about by itinerant pedlars. I recollect one young itinerant vendor of matches, at Llanfyllin, singing out this match song, as he went from door to door:

"Matches - matches - buy my good matches,

They are the best matches that you can desire,

They'll kindle your candle and light your fire;

My father he lies in the sign of the gutter,

And if I don't sell my matches I shall have no supper."

The sign of the gutter alluded to the drunken habits of his ragged parent, who frequently found a lying place in that neighbourhood.

January 9, 1890 *T.W.H.*

Sleepers In Church

It is recorded in a book of 'Clerical Anecdotes' that on the 17th April, 1725, John Rudge bequeathed to the parish of Tryssil, in Shropshire, twenty shillings a year, that a poor man might be employed to go about the church during the sermon and keep the people awake. A bequest by Richard Dovey, of Farmcote, dated 1659, had in view the payment of eight shillings annually to a poor man for the same duties in the church at Clavely, Shropshire. At Acton church, in Cheshire, about thirty years ago, one of the churchwardens or the apparitor used to go round the church during the service, with a long wand in his hand, and if any of the congregation were asleep, they were instantly awoke by a tap on the head.

September 1, 1875 *Nemo.*

The Omen Rod

Dr Owen Pughe in his Dictionary defines the word Coelbren as "a piece of wood used in chusing or balloting, whereon was cut the name of the candidate." My friend, the Rev Owen Jones, Vicar of Pentrevoelas, a parish still somewhat inaccessible (being about seven long steep miles distant from Bettws-y-Coed, the nearest railway station), where old customs and old words are still to be found, informed me that disputants in his parish formerly resorted to the coelbren to settle their differences, presumably small, unimportant matters. This was done as follows:

"A piece of wood, six or so inches long, was dropped by a third party out of his fingers upon a level surface, such as a table, the disputants standing on each side the holder of the wood, and if it fell towards the man on his right, that man won the day, whilst if it fell towards the other party, he was pronounced victor; if the wood even only slightly inclined towards either party that party was declared to be the successful one: if the wood lay equi-distant from both parties the omen rod was again resorted to."

Mr Jones gave a practical illustration of the way in which the ordeal was carried on. The wood was held loosely between his fingers and was dropped vertically onto the table, from which it rebounded, and then fell towards the left. This manner of settling disputes was resorted to in Pentrevoelas, and the neighbouring parishes, up to recent times, and possibly it may even now, in fun rather than in earnest, be used in certain parts of Denbighshire.

April 27, 1887   *E.O.*

Snake Rings

In looking at 'Camden' the other day, to find out what was said about Cerrig-y-Drudion, I found the following in Gibson's additions, which was new to me, "These Druid stones put me in mind of a certain relique of their Doctrine I have lately observed to be yet retain'd amongst the vulgar. For how difficult it is to get rid of such erroneous opinions as have once generally been receiv'd (be they ever so absurd and ridiculous) may be seen at large in the excellent Treatise written upon that subject by Sir Thomas Brown. In most parts of Wales we find it a common opinion of the vulgar, that about Midsummer-Eve (tho' in the time they do not all agree) 'tis usual for snakes to meet in companies, and that by joyning heads together and hissing, a kind of Bubble is form'd like a ring about the head of one of them, which the rest by continual hissing blow on till it comes off at the tail, and then it immediately hardens, and resembles a glass ring; which whoever finds (as some old women and children are persuaded) shall prosper in all his undertakings."

There were plenty of these little rings in existence in Gibson's time. Gibson says they are called "Gleineu Nadroedh" and he conjectures that they were used as "charms and amulets amongst our Druids of Britain."

December 2, 1874   *N.W.S.*

As an instance of the difficulty of getting rid of erroneous opinions, however absurd and ridiculous they may be, I may mention that in the present generation in the centre of Monmouthshire it was, and yet may be at the present time, the belief that snakes were in the habit of meeting in battle, that one or more of their number was killed, and that a "claim" was left upon the scene of the contest. These claims being rare, were highly treasured on account of their virtue in healing wens. My informant states that she knew a woman afflicted with a wen, who for a number of years wore a claim attached to a piece of ribbon around her neck. It was about the size of a walnut. Of course it was only the cast off skin of an ordinary snake. The word "claim" is probably a corruption of the Welsh "glain".

December 23, 1874   *Torfaen*

Many years since one of the gamekeepers of Llangedwyn Hall informed me that he was once much frightened on Midsummer Eve at Tanygraig Wood by witnessing many snakes joining heads and making a hideous noise, and that they were in the habit of leaving a ring behind, which was considered lucky to have. I have heard a similar story of one Evan, a keeper at Llwyn, Llanfyllin, about seventy years ago, coming across a large number of snakes at the Derwlwyn, which was a notorious place for them, in a similar position, and he had to run away, as they were on the point of setting on him! An elderly person in Yale told me the other day that she wore what they called a snake-ring stone round her neck when a child, to prevent having the whooping cough and other epidemics, and that it was a common habit in Yale amongst the inhabitants in those days.

May 30, 1888   *Llywarch Hen*

The Invisible Riders

Not long ago I caught a young colt for the purpose of "breaking it in". A servant who was assisting observed, "They have been riding this one right enough." I asked, "Who?" He replied, "Well, the fairies." "How do you know?" I asked him again. "Don't you see how they have plaited the mane?" he replied; "they always do that when they have a ride." Oddly enough the mane was plaited in a wonderfully artistic manner.

October 25, 1893   *T.H.J.*

A farm servant told me that many years ago he had seen a horse going at a tremendous pace in a circle on a field belonging to Llwydiarth, in the parish of Llanfihangel yng Ngwynfa, Montgomeryshire. It was late at night, and he and his companions had gone to the house courting. But as they had a very poor reception, in going away they turned into the field to see what was the matter with the horse. With difficulty they captured and led him out of the ring. The horse then seemed much relieved, and in a short time began grazing, but they could not get him to go near the circle. My informant believed that one of the fairies was riding the horse.

April 10, 1895   *C.A.*

The belief in Fairies as Jockeys is, or rather was, a very common belief in Monmouthshire. I have heard my grandfather say that it was the usual custom to place a peg cut out of a Rowan or mountain ash tree on the yoke worn by the oxen, to prevent the witches from riding them.

January 8, 1896   *W.H.*

In Shropshire the invisible riders are not fairies, but witches. A man from the neighbourhood of the Brown Clee Hills between Bridgnorth and Ludlow — the highest hills in the county — told me the following tale, about twenty years ago:

There was a waggoner who, when he went into the stable to give the horses their supper, used to find them in a lather, although the day's work had been finished hours before. Unable to account for it, he consulted a "wise woman", who told him to watch, as a witch had been riding them. He failed to detect anything, but, at last, noticed a bit of straw on one of the horses. He took it, and having said a charm which he had learnt from the old woman, threw it on the fire, when the witch was seen disappearing up the chimney.

In some districts, when horses' manes have tangled locks they are called "witches' stirrups".

April 24, 1895   *R.E.D.*

The mane and tail of a colt or horse in "lying out" get into such a tangled mess of knots and twists that it is impossible to unravel them without the aid of a sharp pointed knife to cut through them.

December 23, 1896   *J.J.*

Witch Refused Chips

Many years ago, a publican at Llanfyllin, who was suffering severely from erysipelas in his knee, believed that he had been witched by an elderly widow, who was then residing "in that peaceful little town". All the doctors in the neighbourhood tried their best to alleviate his pains, but without success. He could not banish from his mind the appearance of the old lady when he refused giving her chips, and continued to believe that she was the cause of all his sufferings.

However, at last, a small farmer in the neighbourhood was sent to "Shon Gyfarwydd, the wise astrologer of Llanbrynmair", who, in the language of Shakespeare, could
"Call spirits from the vasty deep."
The farmer, after gravely consulting the oracle, returned, when a cockerel was immediately procured, and was tied in his feathers around the sufferer's knee. They afterwards sent for the old woman Price to give her blessings in their doings. The bird was kept on the joiner's knee for several days without effecting a cure. The patient was taken afterwards to Shrewsbury Infirmary, where death put an end to his misery and superstition.

August 8, 1883   (*From 'Cymru Fu' - Ed.*)

The Vengeful Spirit

At one time a branch of the Devereux family lived at Bryn-glas Hall, three miles north of Llanfair, and the ghost (yspryd) that I am now going to speak about was the bane of existence to this Bryn-glas branch of the family for a considerable time. The ghost made its appearance in the woods and hedge-row on the road-side near the house, in the form of a flickering light, and was always in the way when the master of Bryn-glas came home from Pool or Llanfair. It always uttered in a dismal tone the warning and prophetic words "Dial daw, Dial daw" ("Vengeance will come"). It was believed that its mission and the burden of its speech had reference directly to Squire Devereux, who, like other Welsh gentlemen of his day, partook of the good things of this life "not wisely but too well" — in fact this particular squire never quitted Llanfair town of nights without being more or less in a state of intoxification. This yspryd then had a special mission to perform (so the neighbours imagined), and if only someone would speak to it (they argued), and ask its message it would never more trouble the neighbourhood.

Now, it is said, Squire Devereux at last mastered courage to do this piece of business himself, first fortifying himself for the task by sundry potations in the town, and thus equipped, he went full of courage to the terrible thing, and asked for an explanation. But the apparition was too much for his nerves, and his voice gave way and all he could say in reply to the dreaded "Dial daw" was "Pa bryd?" ("When?") in a very hoarse whisper: to which the spirit replied, "Yn amser y gorwyrion y daw ("in the days of the great grandchildren it will come"). The voice after this was heard no more. It has been maintained that the prediction uttered by the yspryd really did come to pass; and that with the fourth generation died the Devereux family of Bryn-glas.

February 18, 1903   *R.O.*

Prior to "R.O's" highly interesting contribution I was certainly under the impression that I was the only individual living who had either heard of or knew anything about the Bryn-glas ghost. It is really almost incredible, this sudden and unexpected resuscitation of a defunct "yspryd", or rather of its exploits. In this connection I may mention that my father in the early part of his career, took up his residence at Bryn-glas, jointly, it is assumed, with the Devereuxes, being, I believe, in no way related to them.

This was evidently at a period when the manifestations of the supposed ghost were at their height, for by day as well as by night, the mansion was being subjected to intermittent storms of missiles, but whence they came or by whom or what sped, remained undiscovered, and apparently undiscoverable. Many's the night that my father, armed to the teeth on detection bent, kept vigil in an adjoining orchard, but on these particular nights neither goblin, ghost or demon incarnate deigned, or more probably, dared to put in an appearance, or continue the molestations.

A certain yokel, whose veracity was regarded as unimpeachable, protested that at midday, in the light of the sun, he had seen the body of a waggon make a complete revolution, the wheels meanwhile remaining stationary; but to the credit to the less superstitious be it recorded that this business was accepted *cum grando*. It may, however, interest the curious to be informed that the exit of the Devereuxes and my father — *de mortuis nil nisi bonum* — and that of the ghost, appear to have synchronised, or very nearly so, in a remarkable manner, so that the light which was then

18

beginning to beat down on the dark corners of Wales penetrated even the once haunted halls of Bryn-glas.

March 4, 1903   *M. D. Jones, Berriew Endowed School*

I have read with extreme interest the paragraphs relative to "Yspryd Bryn-glas". I have been acquainted with the story of the Yspryd these thirty years, my father having related it to me as long as that ago. Indeed, the Yspryd Bryn-glas has had for us a terrible significance, much as we, and I especially, feign to disbelieve in all matters superstitious; but in "R.O's" account of the Yspryd, I hear for the first time of its colloquy with John Devereux. My grandfather, after his marriage to Miss Williams, of Llangyniew Rectory, lived for some years at Bryn-glas Hall, being at that time a man of considerable means, and heir presumptive to the Garth-lwyd Estates, his uncle, Mr Lloyd, having bred him in this belief, and he having lived at Garth-lwyd from childhood.

Directly he took up his residence at Bryn-glas, strange phenomena manifested themselves, and the family was very much disturbed in consequence. My grandfather kept watch repeatedly in the full assurance, he being anything but a superstitious man, that the disturbances were caused by persons of malicious of mischievous intent, but ultimately he adopted a different view and became profoundly impressed by something which took place and of which only he had cognisance.

I have always understood that the curse "Dial daw" was pronounced on my grandfather and his immediate descendants, and certain it is with the single exception of my own father not one escaped the ban. The Far West, the battlefields of America, South Africa long years ago, each and all claimed a victim, and some died in absolute want and ignominy at our very doors. Disaster upon disaster speedily followed the pronouncement "Dial daw". Mr Lloyd was gathered to his fathers and laid to rest midst solemn pomp and sable woe, the tenanty was gathered together, as the custom then was, the will was read and lo! in the place of the name John Jones appeared that of Frederick Jones, his cousin.

Five and twenty years ago, as a boy, I was walking to Welshpool, when an old man overtook me: he stopped and asked me if I belonged to the Garth-lwyd Family. I told him I believed so. He said, "I see the likeness", and then, taking me by the arm — "Young man, I knew your grandfather, there is a curse on him and all belonging to him."

April 1, 1903   *M.W.J., Oxford*

Hell Of A Performance

In *Bardd Cwsg* (first edition, 1703,p131) occurs a passage which may be thus translated:

"Here is a fellow who has been making a great fool of himself, as the Devil did at Shrewsbury the other day, who in the midst of the interlude of Doctor Faustus . . . made his appearance to play his own part, by which blunder, he drove every one from taking his pleasure to praying."

April 26, 1876   *Cochwilliad*

Faith Out Of Hand

The *Salopian Journal* of Sep 24, 1800, tells the story of a man at Market Drayton who, having bought a few pounds of rags on the Sabbath day, was told it had been better for him to have cut off his right hand, and cast it from him, than to have committed such an act. The man accordingly went home, and by dint of a good deal of hard chopping managed to sever his hand from his arm just above the wrist, and then, with his left hand to cast from him the offending member. A second amputation became necessary, which the surgeon who was called in was compelled to make above the elbow. The man was reported as likely to recover, and full of the belief he had done his duty.

January 11, 1882   *Gleaner*

Turnip Points The Finger

The *Monmouthshire Merlin*, somewhere about the year 1832, narrated a wonderful story of a turnip. At the time the paragraph appeared, a man had plucked a turnip in crossing a field, which, to his astonishment, resembled in shape a man's right hand, minus the thumb. This he exhibited in Monmouth, and it was said that half a dozen years before, the body of a man named Gurney, a toll-gate keeper, had been found barbarously murdered in a turnip field near Ledbury. The unfortunate man, in his agonies, had grasped his hands full of the green tops of the turnips. A waggoner, named Powell, an athletic man, and who had by accident lost his right thumb, was apprehended on suspicion of being concerned in the murder, but for lack of evidence was discharged, and he left the country.

From that year to the one in which the oddly shaped turnip was plucked, the field had not been sown with turnips, and it was said that the man (a servant of Mr J. Biddulph's) who pulled it out of the ground, did so in the very spot where Gurney's murdered body was found, and to the astonishment and dismay of his neighbours it was found to resemble the hand of Powell even down to a wart upon one of the fingers.

April 12, 1876   *O.S.S.B.*

A Bright Spark

Among the many forms of celebrating the Diamond Jubilee, beacon fires have been one. On Jubilee Day, 1887, thirty-four were distinctly visible from the top of Black Hill, Newtown, including several in Merioneth and Salop.

On the marriage of the Prince of Wales in March, 1863, a huge pile of cordwood had been erected on a hill not a hundred miles from Newtown, and to add to its inflammability sundry barrels of pitch and tar had been incorporated, and I believe paraffin and turpentine had been largely used for the same purpose. However, a very clever and able, but eccentric, doctor, who was one of the prime movers of the whole affair, had still some misgivings on the point, so, to make assurance double sure, he went up on the morning of the memorable day and applied a match to a corner of the pile just to see if it would burn! In an instant the whole fabric was enveloped in flame, and before noon all was over — nothing was left but a few handfuls of ashes. The dismay of the poor doctor may be more easily imagined than described.

June 23, 1897   *R.W.*

Tat In Wills

There is always something interesting and instructive in old Wills, the subject of the fifth chapter [of the Cardiff Corporation issue of old records, edited by archivist Mr John Hobson Matthews]. Mr Matthews remarks upon the minuteness with which ancient testators disposed of their personal effects, including, it will be seen, "old" clothes and the suit in wear when the will was made:

"Anne Evans, a widow, leaves James Evans a chaff bed, 'with my ould petticott and wascott to his wiefe.' 'Item, I give and bequeath unto William Richards of Cardiff my late husband's best breeches.'

"Robert Yeorath in 1706 bequeaths to sister Mary 'a black Cow, her name is Blacky. Item, I gives and bequeath to John Rosser a suit of Cloaths that I wear every day. Item, I gives and bequeath to Abigail Rosser her grandmother's Bed when she does marrie.'

"Another debtor leaves to niece Mary John 'my best Hatt and black Napkin and a feather Pillow and all ye bees that is between She and I.' "

December 24, 1901   *Ed.*

An Impudent Prisoner

At the Chester Assizes, August, 1825, William Leighton, for picking pockets at Congleton, was sentenced to be transported for life. On sentence being passed, the prisoner in the most audacious manner, called out to the Judge, and, snapping his fingers, said, "I'll toss you, hang or quits."

March 18, 1885   *Ed.*

Christmas Customs

I remember being told by an octogenarian, lately deceased, of the observance of a peculiar Christmas custom — the only example which has come under my notice. When young, she was engaged as domestic servant

at a farmhouse in the parish of Bettws-Cedewen. On getting up one Christmas morning she found the breakfast table already laid in a sumptuous manner, an unusual occurence. When her master and mistress came down, she applied to them for an explanation, and was informed that it was done to give welcome to Joseph and Mary to the house.

January 26, 1887   *T.H.J.*

On Christmas morn the cattle that had previously been fed on straw each had a foddering of best hay, and it was said that if anyone was impious enough to stay up on Christmas Eve and watch till midnight they would find the cows all upon their knees; but something was sure to happen to those who were guilty of such temerity.

January 6, 1897   *J.J.*

I know a Shropshire farmer who never allows his horses to be worked from Christmas Eve till New Year's Day. His workmen feed them, and the cattle and sheep, morning and evening, but are allowed to have the rest of the days for themselves for any purpose they choose.

Deecember 30, 1908   *J.H.C.*

A correspondent in the *Oswestry Advertizer* in Sep 1858 said, upon Christmas-days, about three o'clock in the morning, most of the parishioners used to assemble in Welsh churches, and after prayers and a sermon continue singing psalms and hymns with great devotion till broad day; and if, through age or infirmity, any were disabled from attending, they never failed having prayers at home, accompanied with carols on our Saviour's nativity. The former part of this custom is still observed, but is too often perverted by intemperence. This act of devotion is called 'Plygain', or the crowing of the cock. It has been a general belief among the superstitious that, instantly, on hearing that shrill sound

"— Whether in sea or fire, in earth or air,

Th' extravagant and erring spirit hies

To his confine."

And during the whole Christmas season the cock was supposed to exert his powers throughout the night; from which undoubtedly originated the Welsh word Plygain, as applied to this custom. Shakespeare finely described this old opinion in 'Hamlet' act 1, scene 1.

January 3, 1877   *Nemo*

On Christmas Eve a number of [Oswestry] men got a handbarrow, of their own making, on which they laid a bed of clay about an inch in thickness, and in this clay they made a number of holes for the reception of candles in the form of a star. The candles, I believe, were the savings of some previous months of the "ends" unburnt in the pits. The 'Star of Bethlehem', as they called it, two of them carried from house to house, a third carrying a light in a lantern, for their 'star' was only illuminated while they were exhibiting it. Sometimes, but not always, they sang a carol; and having collected their Christmas boxes, moved onto the next house of call. I have never seen any but colliers carry these candles, and always at Christmas, though I have heard that they do so sometimes on Hallow Eve and Candlemas.

June 24, 1874   *Ben Starch*

The Colliers from the Drill have not given up this old custom. They still light their candles and sometimes sing a carol at Morda at Christmas.

June 24, 1874   *W.H.*

The custom of carrying lighted candles by the colliers was until lately observed in the neighbourhood of St Martins, where it is called The Star.

When the men arrive at a house they kneel round their star and say a carol.
June 24, 1874   *J. Jones, Wootton*

The Rev D. Sylvan Evans writes to the Academy: "Something similar to the 'hunting of the wren' was not unknown in the Principality as late as a century ago, or later. In the Christmas holidays, it was the custom of young men, not necessarily boys, to visit the abodes of such couples as had been married within the year. The order of the night — for it was strictly a nightly performance — was to this effect.

"Having caught a wren, they placed it on a miniature bier made for the occasion, and carried it in procession towards the house which they intended to visit. Having arrived they serenaded the master and mistress of the house under their bedroom window with the following doggerel:

'Dyma'r dryw
Os yw e'n fyw,
I gael ei rostio.'

That is, 'Here is the wren, if it is alive, or a sparrow to be roasted.' If they could not catch a wren for the occasion, it was lawful to substitute a sparrow (aderyn to).

"The husband, if agreeable, would then open the door, admit the party, and regale them with plenty of Christmas ale, the obtaining of which being the principle object of the whole performance. The company then departed in a merry mood. Other houses in the district, similarly circumstanced, would be visited on subsequent night until the Epiphany, which was called 'distyll y gynliau,' or ebb of the holidays, when all festivities connected with Christmas terminated.

"I ought to have mentioned that if the wren-party were not admitted into the house and entertained, in parting they gave vent to their feeling of disappointment in the following malediction:

'Gwynt ffralwm
Ddelo'n hwthwm
I droi'r tŷ
A'i wyneb fyny.'

Which may be translated —

'Come raging wind, in fury frown,
And turn the house all upside down."
April 22, 1885   *Ed.*

In 'Folk-Lore', vol.4 p122, an account is given of a custom which prevailed in South Wales in recent years; it is remembered by Principal Viriamu Jones of the University College at Cardiff. Towards the end of the year — some say the last day of November, others say nearer Christmas — the white horse was taken round the parish. A framework in the shape of a horse's head was covered with white drapery, which fell like a sheet over the body of the boy on whom it was placed. Some of the heads had jaws which could be opened and shut. 'The horse' was led by a young man or youth, and used to frighten children and young women, so successfully sometimes, that it is said the practice was put down at Whitland because of the terror it occasioned.

March 27, 1895   *W.O.*

I have found in *Cymru Fu* the following details, additional to those which have already appeared in your columns:

"The horse was accompanied by two characters, known as 'Pwnsh and Shaun', both in ragged, dirty clothes, and masked, the former carrying a staff, the latter a broom, with which they poke the fire and sweep the hearth. This was probably an attack on the hearth, of the same nature as that described by Miss Burne in her *Shropshire Folk-lore*, where the character is called 'Little Jack Dont'. As 'Pwnsh and Shaun' appear in only this one account, it is quite possible they are not original features of the Mari Lwyd. The performance seems to be a South Wales feature; at present I have met with it in the following localities: Cowbridge, the Swansea Valley, Sketty, near Swansea, Llendebie: it is important to note that at the last place a horse's skin actually figured. The origin of the name Mari Lwyd is unknown; the connection with the procession with the Virgin Mary is certainly not obvious. It seems most probable that it was a mid-winter ceremony baptized with an ecclesiastical title.

January 1, 1896   *N.W.T.*

"In the county of Hereford some of the old ceremonies are yet (1840) practised. On the eve of Old Christmas Day there are thirteen fires lighted in the cornfields of many farms, twelve of them in a circle, and one round a pole, much larger and higher than the rest, and in the centre. The fires are dignified with the names of the Virgin Mary and twelve Apostles, the lady being in the middle; and while they are burning the labourers retire into some shed or outhouse, where they behold the brightness of the apostolic flame. In this shed they lead a cow on whose horns a large plum-cake has been stuck, and having assembled round the animal, the oldest labourer takes a pail of cider, and addresses the following lines to the cow with great solemnity:

'Here's to thy pretty face and thy white horn,
God send thy master a good crop of corn,
Both wheat, rye and barley, all sorts of grain,
And next year, if we're alive, we'll drink to thee again.'

After which the verse is chanted in chorus by all present. They then dash the cider in the cow's face, when, by a valiant toss of her head, she throws the plum-cake on the ground; and if it falls forward, it is an omen that the next harvest will be good; if backward, that it will be unfavourable. This is the commencement of the rural feast, which is generally prolonged to the following morning."

The Mirror.

October 5, 1892   *B.*

Archdeacon Howell, writing in the *Cyfaill Eglwysig* on Welsh customs in the Vale of Glamorgan, says:

"Much importance was attached to the Twelfth Night in ancient times. I remember it was the custom in the Vale of Glamorgan to prepare a big loaf, or, rather, a pile of cakes in farm-houses against the Epiphany, and many harmless ceremonies were practised on the feast. The old people, who clung to ancient customs, used to divide the cake, in a figurative sense, between Christ, the Virgin Mary, the Magi (or wise men), and the company.

"It was on this night (the Twelfth) in some places formerly the king of the neighbourhood was elected. The King and Queen of Misrule were elected by concealing a ring in the cake and whoever got the ring was chosen.

"A log of wood was placed on the fire of sufficient size to last for twelve days and twelve nights. This, probably, was the origin of the Yule Log. It was at this season the Druids used to cut the mistletoe and divide it between the tribes, and the branches were kept carefully in the houses throughout the season, in order to ensure success and safety. And this, may be, was the origin of the custom of decorating houses with holly against Christmas, and the evergreens were not removed before the Epiphany."

August 26, 1896   *W.O.*

Visitors' Books

In the Visitors' Book, at the Llewellyn Arms at this place [Beddgelert], some wandering cockney, evidently out without a guide, and agitated with the poetic phrenzies engendered by the air of the Welsh mountains, asks the question:

"Where is Snowden? please to say,
When you next shall pass this way;
'Mongst the mountains it ranks high,
I fear it's nearer Heav'n than I."

To which some kindred bard, better read in Welsh topography and celestial affinities, has favour'd Welsh tourists with the following exact information:

"On referring to my Diary,
I can answer this inquiry;
Snowden hence, is North, by West,
The biggest and the best,
When you are on its highest bit,
Then you'll be nearer Heav'n than it."

September 9, 1874 *Nemo*

Most tourists to Beddgelert I suppose go to see the so-called grave of the hound and a goodly number seem to record their impressions in the Visitors' books of the hotels they stop at. The other day I had occasion to make my temporary abode the very comfortable house the Saracen's Head, and in looking over the book in the Coffee Room I found the following:

"I came to weep at Gelert's grave, but found the skies before
Had washed it so, I feared myself to wash it anymore;
Ah! 'lucky dog!' if such the state of sweet Beddgelert's weather,
I fear you are ne'er unwept for many hours together!"

Another tourist also records his impressions in a verse to the following effect:

"Under the shadow of Moel Hebog
    Lies buried Llewellyn's faithful dog,
In a fit of anger one day he stuck it
For he fancied the child had kicked the bucket,
    So he reverently buried the bones
And to show he repented put up these stones."

I am not aware that history records that the Goat hotel was erected on the site where Llewellyn's child was eventually buried, but a more recent tourist has added to the verse the following: "P.S. — And they put up the 'Goat' where they buried the 'Kid'.

September 14, 1881   *G.G.*

Here are a few lines I found at or near Pentre Voelas:

"Pentre Voelas, Pentre Voelas,

Half thy joys have not been told us,

Thou canst cure when sickness holds us

Better than a doctor's bolus."

August 22, 1877   *G.D.L.*

The following I copied about the year 1850, at the Havod Hotel, Devil's Bridge:

"Oh! Cambria dear Cambria tho'rough are thy roads

Yet this place makes ample amends:

If the devil thus furnishes all his abodes

No wonder he has many friends."

July 21, 1875   *J.W.B.*

In the three verses by the three friends, 'C.K.', 'T.T.' and 'T.H.' [Charles Kingsley, Thomas Hughes and Tom Taylor], at Penygwryd, one runs as follows:

"T.H.

Oh my dear namesake's breeches, you never see the like,

He bust them all so shameful a crossing of a dyke,

But Mrs Owen patched them as careful as a mother,

With flannel of three colours — she hadn't got no other."

August 11, 1875   *G.G.*

Toads In Stones

It may interest some of your numerous readers to learn that about three years ago, when the workmen at the Sweeney Clay Quarry were engaged in clearing the soil, gravel, &c, from the surface of the clay, they came upon a large boulder, weighing about 12 cwt, too large to be moved without breaking. When it was broken, judge of the men's surprise to see

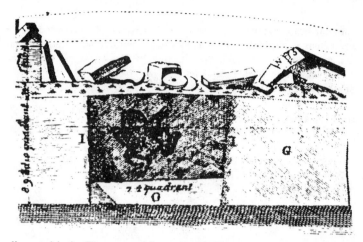

a live toad in it. The present foreman, Mr Evans, can corroborate this.
May 28, 1902   *R.W.*

A few days ago while blasting the rock in sinking a well at the steam
laundry, Victoria-road, Chester, the men at work came upon a live toad at
a depth of 25 yards 2 feet from the surface. The well is sunk in rock.
June 27, 1888   *Ed.*

The following is extracted from *Notes and Queries* for March, 1856:

"Perhaps the following notice of the discovery of a toad at considerable
depth may not be unacceptable to some readers of *Notes and Queries*,
the more so as the particulars of such events have generally been very
vaguely described. Hearing that a living toad had been dug up near the
village of Benthall, near Bosely, in Shropshire, on September 23, last, and
being in the neighbourhood, I walked over on March 21 and had the
pleasure of making his acquaintance. His present possessor and
discoverer, Mr Bathurst, a manufacturer of earthenware at Benthall, who
had taken great interest in the subject, courteously gave me a minute
description of the 'find', and took me to see the exact spot. He assured me
that his father, who was present at the exhumation, and himself had
carefully, but vainly, sought for any fissure in the superincumbent strata
through which the animal could have crawled or fallen, and my own
examination, which was a leisurely one, also failed in detecting any.

"The total depth was five feet six or seven inches from the surface, and the order of the strata as shown by a perpendicular section is as follows: first, the turf of the meadow, resting upon a bed of clay mixed with gravel, beneath which was a thickness of three feet clay, lying upon a stratum of ferruginous coal of the inferior kind used in the kilns. This was a foot thick, and immediately beneath was a bed of what is technically called 'tough clay'. This was of a light buff colour, and is used for making chimney pots and coarser yellow basins. It is almost as tenacious as putty, and in this, at a depth of sixteen inches below the coal, the toad was found in a matrix fitting his body as closely as wax does the seal. The spade, fortunately, brought up the clod without injury to its inhabitant.

"As might be expected, for some time he was very impatient of light, which appeared to distress him greatly, but by degrees he became accustomed to it. When I saw him his eyes were as brilliant as possible, his skin moist and of a full olive green, and his mouth hermetically sealed. These are the facts upon which I shall make no comment, simply vouching for those I myself noted; and observing that those respecting the 'find' itself are above suspicion, from the known character of the Messrs Bathurst in the vicinity."

May 21, 1902   *W. J. Bernard Smith*

The Horned Woman

Margaret Griffith, wife of David Owen, of "Llan Gaduain", Montgomeryshire, was shown in London, because a crooked horn, four inches long, grew out of the middle of her forehead! A pamphlet, giving "a miraculous and monstrous, but most true and certain account" of her, with a rude portrait affixed, was "imprinted at London by Thomas Owen, in the year of the Spanish Armada, and sold by Edward White at the little north door of St Paul's Church, at the sign of the Gun."

November 14, 1876   *Eliola*

A Cheap Bargain

A newspaper of April, 1815, says that William Jones, a pauper, aged 79, who had been married only three weeks, sold his wife for three-half-pence in the market place at Llanrwst.

October 23, 1878   *Ed.*

Child Brides

Mr J. P. Earwaker brought a very curious phase of the social life of bygone Cheshire before the last meeting of the Lancashire and Cheshire Antiquarian Society. In 1562 Margery Vernon, between the age of nine and ten, was married to Randle More, who was two years younger. In another case Isabel Orrell deposes that she cannot perfectly remember her marriage, but knows by credible report that it was celebrated in Turton Chapel when she was seven years old, and when her bridegroom was of the age of five or six. When Gilbert Gerrard and Emma Tabot were married at Leigh Church the boy's uncle held up the bridegroom, who was five years old, and "spake the words of matrimony for the child's part, and the woman" — who was six years of age — "spake for herself as she was taught."

In another case the bridegroom was bribed to go to church by the present of an apple! John Rigmarden at the age of three was married to a bride of five. He was carried in the arms of a clergyman, who coaxed him to repeat the words of matrimony. Before he had got through his lesson the child declared he would learn no more that day. The priest answered. "You must speak a little more, then go play you."

A daughter of Sir William Brereton was married at the age of two to a husband who was a year older than herself. Both the children were of course carried in the arms of elders, who spoke for them after the fashion of sponsors at the baptismal font. "This," one of the witnesses remarked, "was the youngest marriage ever he was at."

If there was no ratification of the marriage when years of consent were attained — twelve for the girl and fourteen for the boy, it might be dissolved. Otherwise it was customary though not essential to ratify the matrimonial contract in a public and ceremonious manner.

March 18, 1885   *Ed.*

Flower Folklore

A curious superstition prevails in Castle Caereinion parish that if a daffodil is brought into a house where a goose is sitting nothing will come of the eggs — that the whole sitting will be a failure. Time was when hens, and ducks, and geese, and their sittings, were beset with many difficulties, consequent upon the superstitions of the people.

July 20, 1892 *E.O.*

A young man entered a cottage at Kinnerley a few days ago wearing a daffodil in his buttonhole. A daughter had tried to refuse him admission because of him wearing the flower, and the mother, coming in, exclaimed — "For God's sake, take that flower out of your coat, I have a hen sitting on duck eggs!" The same superstition is believed in in Montgomeryshire. In the parish of Kerry, a day or two ago, a cottager's wife told another that she would never rear some chickens that she had unless a jar of daffodils that was in the window was removed.

April 28, 1897 *W.M.*

It is considered unlucky to carry the catkins of the hazel or the willow into a farmhouse in the spring, as there will then be no Goslings or young Lambs.

May 9, 1894 *J.*

A contributor of *Notes and Queries* says in Shropshire it is considered unlucky to bring snowdrops into the house. Another contributor says it is unlucky for a woman to present them or bring them into the house.

May 8, 1895 *W.O.*

The writer took into his house a couple of bunches of hawthorn twigs, one, with purple double blossoms, and the other with single red blossoms, two very beautiful sprigs, but instead of being thanked, he was greeted with the remark, "Why do you bring those shocking things into the house, do you not know it is very unlucky to bring them into a house?" He did not know this, and to save other thoughtless, ignorant people like himself from committing such a terrible blunder, he sends this note to *Bye-Gones* to warn them, and to tell them not to take ill luck into their houses in the month of May by carrying hawthorn blossoms. It is much better to secure good luck than to carry pretty hawthorn blossoms about the country!

May 17, 1893 *Blodwel*

I am well accustomed to the idea of it being unlucky to bring hawthorn into the house. I do not remember hearing of it west of Shrewsbury, but I think that it is a general belief in South Shropshire, though not on the

Worcestershire border. The strong scent is apt to be overpowering, and to cause headaches, so that the dislike of bringing branches indoors is founded on stern common-sense.

July 15, 1914   *A.*

The superstition that it is considered unlucky to take the hawthorn, ie, I suppose, the May blossom, into the house, is rampant at and about Bangor. Several times last year I carried home bunches of such blossom, and on the way home, and in the home itself I was warned — not always seriously — of the results that might happen. About the same time I happened to be visiting Haverfordwest, Pembrokeshire, and heard that the same superstition exists in that county.

September 1, 1915   *T. Witton Davies*

The Cardeus Benedictus (Blessed Thistle) is called the "Virgin Mary's Thistle", and the white spots on the leaves are said to have been caused by the Blessed Virgin, when suckling the Divine Infant, letting some of her milk fall on the plant. It is considered unlucky to kill one of the plants.

Midsummer Rose. I do not know the generic name of this rose. It bears a very small double flower, nearly mauve in colour. I know of only two places where it grows — one garden in Tong and one in Tong Norton. It used to be believed that if a maiden would gather an opening bud of this rose very early on Midsummer Day, and seal it up in a white package and wish for a husband, she would have an offer of marriage before the year was out. I almost think I have also heard it called "Maiden's Blush."

July 23, 1913   *J. H. Clarke*

The name of Virgin Mary's Thistle for the Blessed Thistle is recorded in Cheshire, but not in Shropshire, but with a different legend from that quoted by Mr Clarke. In that legend its leaves were used by the Virgin Mary, with other remedies, to keep away evil influences from the sick. In Suffolk yet another different legend is attached to it. There the Virgin is said to have formed of its broad leaf a vessel into which to milk a cow, and with that the plant should thenceforth retain the marks which the leaf used had then received. In the 'Shropshire Word Book' Miss Jackson records Virgin Mary's Honeysuckle for the common Lungwort (*Pulmonaria officinalis*) and quotes a Welshampton woman's authority for attaching to that plant the legend which Mr Clarke has heard applied to the Thistle. At Welshampton it was explained that "the leaves (of the Lungwort) have been spotted ever since."

The name of Maiden's Blush is applied to more than one variety of the Rosa alba type. The original type, in cultivation since the close of the 16th century, bears small, white, fragrant blooms. The varieties are described as bearing blush or rosy-tinted blooms of great fragrance. One now in bloom in my garden has white outer petals with a bright pink centre, the blooms being about two inches in diameter.

August 20, 1913   *O.Y.*

Dick Spot The Conjuror

There is in the British Museum a pamphlet entitled 'The / Life / and / mysterious transactions / of / Richard Morris, Esq., / better known by the name of / Dick Spot the conjuror / particularly in Derbyshire and Shropshire / written by an old acquaintance who was a critical observer of all his actions for neare fifty years,' &c. London 1798. Author not named.

In it is stated that Richard Morris was born at Bakewell in Derbyshire in 1710. The name "Dick Spot" was given to him from his having "from birth a black spot on his face near his nose. His father was a soldier at the time of the union and died before Dick had completed his sixth year. By his mother he was nearly related to the late Sir Richard Arkwright, the greatest mechanic in the Kingdom; and by his father he also claimed relationship to the founder of the Soho Manufactory.

"Mrs Morris survived her husband but two years and left her son to her sister Deborah Heathcote, who gave him as good a learning as her circumstances would permit, which though not affluent, was liberal, enough to give him an introduction to any business he might have an indication for. Dick certainly during the time of his being at school applied his talents to a good purpose for he was much the best calculator of any man of his aquaintance and his observations of life obviated and removed the necessity of applying to books; for it is a fact that in all his travels he never carried a book not even of roads or directions, but possessed everything as it were by intuitive knowledge . . . His hours of amusement were not spent like those of other children: a sullen and mysterious resolve marked his manners; yet at all times his thoughtfulness would give way to athletic exercise; but this was seldom, for he seemed at most times to be absorbed within himself and would for a long time keep his eyes so fixed upon some inanimate object that observers used to call him 'The Sullen Boy' . . .

"Mrs Heathcote his aunt, who it has been observed was independent in circumstances, contrived to better them by advising the young and amusing the aged in their various concerns in life. The truth is she was a fortune teller; and report declares that she had a happy knack of drawing the secrets of futurity from their hidden recess. From this circumstance Dick might borrow the hint; but he certainly out-ran his aunt as far before he was twelve years old, as a wooden clock is removed from a repeater or a stop-watch though each will declare the time of day. Her fee was constantly half-a-crown; but her nephew never opened his lips before the physician's fee was posted; ie a Guinea."

The tales of which the book is made up have nothing in particular in them. They are much the same as those told of any other conjuror. Dick seems to have had no fixed residence but travelled about from one town to another. His leisure hours "were employed in some mechanism or other. There is a clock of his making at the White Horse at Frankwell in Shrewsbury, which is mostly constructed of wood, in which he has applied an uncommon and very curious escapement and compound pendulum of his own invention. This though a wooden clock scarcely errs a second in the month."

He wrote in the 'Conjuror's Magazine' of Decr. 1791 under 'Notices of January' "The Head of Sweden a cruel and unnatural death." The Magazine was in the hands of the public four clear months before 26th April 1792, "the date of the successful attempt of the regicide Aukerstrom, the news for which was announced on 'Change on the 15th May."

"To those who have a curiosity to hear the history of his last moments I shall just subjoin that exhausted nature ended without a struggle; yet there certainly was heard a very extraordinary rapping against the wainscot of the room he died in and of which he seemed sensible but not affected by it; for when his attendants asked him if he heard the noise behind the wainscot he faintly answered, "Yes," and a little while after he said, "My continuance will be determined by the light of the lamp which will go out before morning," which assuredly came to pass as he said. Thus lived and thus died Richard Morris Esq., at the age of 83, March 4th, 1793, at Oswestry in Shropshire, and on the tenth he was buried in St Mary's Church-yard, Shropshire."

March 27, 1878   *Ap Gwynedd*

In the Rev T. H. Evans's interesting 'History of the Parish of Llanwddyn', we are told that a very mischievous goblin named "Yspryd Cynon" was "put down by 'Dic Spot', and put in a quill, and placed under a large stone in the river."

August 6, 1890 *M.*

In the obituary of the *Gentleman's Magazine* for March 1792, the following brief account of this Oswestry magician is given:

"1792, March 4 — At Oswestry in Shropshire, in the 85th year of his age, Mr Richard Morris, better known by the name of 'Dick Spot the Conjuror', in which profession he was thought by country people to excel most other astrologers. He was a man of no education; but endowed with strong natural abilities, with which he read mankind to some purpose. His person was tall and muscular, with much expression in his marked countenance. He had a dark spot on the side of his face, from whence his nickname took its rise. He was in good credit, and well spoken of by the generality as a good sort of man. He was charitable to the poor. Latterly he was in affluent circumstances, and kept his carriage, when his fee was in all cases a piece of gold, without which he never gave his opinion of stolen property; and it was singular that whenever he gave a favourable answer, it was generally found true; probably from the fear which operates on the mind of the thief, who, in a country place, knowing the verdict of the wise man, and conscious of his guilt, is impelled by fear to restore the property. If this be true may it not be asked, whether a county conjuror is not of more service than a county gaol and a gallows?

"For instance, a gentleman near Shrewsbury in one night lost all his bed and table linen. Morris was then in the town of S. He was fee'd and heard in a grave and fixed attention the short history. 'Sir, there is a person you suspect; but say nothing. Go home, and take no concern about your loss; you will have it all again safe. I cannot tell you how or when; but you will lose nothing.' In about fourteen days, the whole, in a bundle, was found at daylight under his garden-wall."

In an old Welsh book in my possession, published (as far as I can guess) about 1830, at Llanrwst, a number of magic circles and diagrams is said to have been taken from 'The Book of Dick Smot', ie Dick Spot.

July 12, 1912 *H.D.*

Gone Fishing

From Llanmerewig comes the story of the capture of a pike in an extraordinary manner. The other evening the son of Mr Samuel Miller, of The Court, Llanmerewig, set a night-line in a brook near the Court. During the night it appears that a horse came down to the brook at the spot where the line was laid for the purpose of slaking his thirst, never dreaming what excitement was in store for him. By some means he got entangled with the line, and he was struggling to free himself when one of the hooks caught in his tail. He seems at last to have given the matter up as a bad job, and was found next morning with a pike of about three pounds in weight dangling from his tail.

June 1, 1892   *Ed.*

Before the establishment of ironworks on the banks of many of the South Wales streams put an end to the fish, an extraordinary mode of capture was observed. The fishermen commenced operations at the ebbing of the tide by stretching a seine net across the river a few hundred yards from the mouth. Whilst drawing the net towards the sea they incessantly disturbed the water by beating the surface and hurling stones. The affrighted fish naturally made for the sea, which, however, they could not reach except by passing over the intervening low river bar. Here they were pursued by trained dogs, and driven into the hands of the fishermen, who either clubbed, speared, or otherwise caught large quantities of fish.

March 7, 1894   *Devoniensis*

There is a saying in Llanyblodwel parish that the time to begin trout fishing is when the wild pigeon begins cooing. The writer knows nothing of fishing, nor the time when fish are in season, but he knows the cooing is to be heard about the middle of April, and that it is not always heard on the same day. In any case, it is worth recording this bit of folk-lore.

May 5, 1897 *E.O.*

An old man told me lately that when the cattle are grazing the fish are feeding, and that when the cattle are lying down the fish are at the bottom of the streams, chewing the cud, so to speak, and that it is useless fishing for them at such times.

April 12, 1899 *J.A.J.*

About June, 1890, I was fishing on the river Alyn on a warm day, when an old angler came up and used the very same words which "J.A.J." mentions; and he further remarked that the wind from the south blows the bait into the fish's mouth. The latter remark I have often found correct. Another old angler informed me that the fish will never bite when there is thunder about.

April 2, 1902 *J. D. Jones*

The following legend was told me by Mr Griffith Jones of Cae-llwyn-grydd, Llanllechid, Carnarvonshire, and is, I believe still current in the neighbourhood of the River Conway.

In the days of St Ffraid, there was a dire famine in the land and even fish could not be got in sufficient number to allay the hunger of the people. The saint went down to the river, and gathered a quantity of rushes, which she threw into the Conway; and no sooner had the rushes touched the water than they were changed to full-grown fish. The people, seeing the miracle performed, believed it was done for the purpose of supplying them with food; so they caught the fish, cooked, and ate them, and by this means escaped starvation.

I do not know whether the saint continued throwing rushes into the river for some time so as to produce instantaneously a large quantity of fish: my informant spoke of one time only. The fishes, so made, tasted of the rushes out of which they were formed, and in consequence of this taste they were called Brwyniaid, a name they retain to this day. The Welsh for rush is brwyn and hence the pluralised form, Brwyniaid, which may be translated Rushians. The fish are whitish in colour, smaller in size than salmon, larger than herrings. Their English name is sparlings. They frequent the river Conway in the spring for the purpose of spawning. The

time of year when these fish migrate corresponds with Lent, when fish were generally eaten, as well as with that time of the year when food is, or rather was, scarce and dear.

September 28, 1892   *E.O.*

Ghost Harangues Sister

Many years ago two old maiden sisters who were known as Shukan and Bethan lived together at the Oak, a small tenement distant about half a mile from Mochdre Church. In course of time, Shukan, the older of the two, died, and was buried in the Churchyard. It appears she had not been treated kindly, especially during her last illness, by Bethan; and before her departure she declared she would "trouble" her unkind sister.

One night soon afterwards, true to her promise, Shukan appeared at the bedroom window clad in a shroud. She rapped at the window shrieking ever and anon, "Bethan, thee art worse than Judas, Bethan, thee art worse than Judas." Poor Bethan was terrified; and imploringly asked what she should do to get rid of the "trouble".

"Come with me to the Churchyard," was the reply. To this she assented; and hurriedly prepared to accompany her unwelcome visitor. They proceeded on their way. In passing Bron-y-Llan farmhouse, a cock crew; and the ghost of Shukan immediately vanished. Bethan thereupon returned home, to be "troubled" no more;.

September 16, 1891   *T.H.J.*

A Provident Dream

In the *Armenian Magazine* for 1795 is recorded "Mr Boardman's remarkable deliverance". This account was taken from his own lips by Owen Davies at Northampton, on Sep. 7, 1793:

"I preached one evening at Mould in Flintshire, and next morning set out for Park-gate. After riding some miles, I asked a man if I was on my road to that place. He answered: 'Yes, but you will have some sands to go over, and unless you ride very fast, you will be in danger of being enclosed by the tide.' It then began to snow to such a degree, that I could scarce see a step of the way, and my mare being with foal, prevented me from riding so fast as I otherwise should have done. I got to the sands and pursued my journey over them for some time; but the tide then came in and surrounded me on every side, so that I could neither proceed nor return back; and to ascend the perpendicular cliffs was impossible. In this situation I commended my soul to God, not having the least expectation of escaping Death.

"In a little time I perceived two men running down a hill, on the other side of the water, and by some means they got a boat and came to my relief, just as the sea had reached my knees as I sat upon the mare. They took me into the boat, the mare swimming by our side, till we reached land. While we were in the boat one of the men cried out, 'Surely, sir, God is with you.' I answered, 'I trust he is.' The man replied. 'I know he is,' and then related the following circumstance: 'Last night I dreamed I must go the top of such a hill; when I awoke the dream made such an impression on me I coud not rest. I went and called upon this my friend, and desired him to accompany me. When we came to the place we saw nothing more than usual. However, I begged him to go with me to another hill, at a small distance, and there we saw your distressing situation.' "

April 12, 1882   *Nemo*

Model Behaviour

The *British Architect*, apropos of the revival of the art of modelling in wax, reminds us that Hulbert, in his 'Memoirs', records some of the eccentric doings of a gentleman of Moss, who resided at Ringway Outwood, Cheshire, in the early part of the century.

"This gentleman, to make up for want of society, made several wax figures, which were elegantly and fashionably attired, one of which it is said he called Mrs Moss, and at dinner she was placed at the head of the table, the other figures being guests. After dinner they were seated opposite the window, as if observing the passers-by, and many a countryman's bow did these ladies receive, with which Mr Moss was greatly delighted."

August 25, 1880   *Ed.*

Encounters With Fairies

The Rev Peter Roberts in his 'Cambrian Superstitions' refers to the story of a vindictive fairy at Wrexham. Fairies don't like to be stared at. "He who looks on them," says Falstaff, "shall die." The Wrexham Fairy did not go so far, contenting itself with putting out the eyes of the unhappy Wrexhamite. Fancy a blind beggar soliciting charity because the Fairies had destroyed his eyesight!

November 15, 1876   *Taffy*

Mr Hamer's current contribution [to the *Montgomeryshire Collections*] is full of stories of witchcraft and superstition, which make it unusually attractive. We cannot do better than quote one of them, which belongs to quite recent times:

"One Edward Jones, or 'Ned the Jockey', as he was familiarly called, resided, within the memory of the writer, in one of the roadside cottages a short distance from Llanidloes, on the Newtown road. When returning home late one evening it was his fate to fall in with a troop of Fairies, who were not pleased to have their gambols disturbed by a mortal. Requesting him to depart, they politely offered him the choice of the means of locomotion viz., being carried off by a "high wind, middle wind or low wind." The jockey soon made up his mind. No sooner had he given his decision, than he found himself whisked high up into the air, and his senses completely bewildered by the rapidity of his flight: he did not recover himself again till he came to contact with the earth, being suddenly dropped in the middle of a garden near Tŷ Gough, on the Bryndu Road, many miles distant from the spot whence he started on his aerial journey.

"Ned, when relating this story, would vouch for its genuiness in the most solemn manner, and the person who narrated it to the writer brought forward, as a proof of its truth, 'that there was not the slightest trace of any person going into the garden, while Ned was found in the middle of it'. The ultimate fate of the hero of the above incident was extremely melancholy. Returning home inebriated one night, he appears to have mistaken his road, and walked into the Severn, just below Long Bridge, where his body was found next morning."

November 14, 1877   *Ed.*

An old friend, who is laden with recollections of former days, told me the following tale:

A good while ago a cottager lived in a small house in a place called Bwlch-y-ddar, a hamlet between Llangedwyn and Llanfyllin. His name was Robert Jones. He lived alone. His landlord was Col Bonnor's grandfather, a gentleman who was loved by his tenants, and consulted by them in matters of importance. With this introduction what follows become legible.

"One night Robert Jones was aroused from a refreshing sleep by a noise in his room. He sat up in his bed and saw a small man fiddling like mad, seated on the post of the bed, and small men and women dancing all about the room in great glee. For awhile he looked on with wonder, and at last he said, with something like a Welsh oath, "Who are you?" The little fiddler, with merriment in his twinkling eyes, said, "We are the spirits of the air" (ysprydion yr awyr).

"But what do you want here?"

"Only a dance, and we are going to come here tomorrow night, too."

"No, you won't," said Robert Jones, and he added, with something more like an oath than any other kind of expression, "I tell you, you won't. Mr Bonnor shall be told of this, and then none of you dare."

This threat was quite enough for the intruders, and Robert Jones was never disturbed afterwards. All this took place towards the early part of the present century.

January 4, 1899   *E.O.*

In a very curious work 'A relation of Apparitions of Spirits in the county of Monmouth and the Principality of Wales', by the Rev Edmund Jones of the Trench, we meet with what is termed an excellent way of getting rid of a fairy:

"C.T. (a person of strict veracity) travelling by night over Bedwellty mountain towards the valley of Ebwy Fawr, was surrounded by fairies, some dancing, and heard the sound of a bugle horn like persons hunting. He then began to be afraid, but recollected having heard that if any person should happen to see the fairies, if he drew his knife they would vanish directly, he did so, and saw them no none!"

May 13, 1885 *Verax*

Music heard in the night, in places remote from human abodes, such as wild moorlands, is generally ascribed to the Fairies. I lately heard two such instances of nocturnal music, which I give just as I heard them related to me by a clergyman, who has been vicar of his present upland parish for twenty years. The first tale was told my friend by a parishioner who is still alive. It is as follows:

"The vicar's informant was a woman who had paid a visit to a sick friend and was returning home along a lonely footpath, which was pointed out to me, close to a wood, and as she was approaching the sideland she heard charming music, much like that produced by numerous small, silvery bells. Her path lay close to the spot whence the music was proceeding, and when she was within thirty yards of the hollow in the field where it was, she stopped and listened to the sweet sounds; but she had not long been there before a something came running forwards from the direction of the hollow, and brushed past her, and struck against her as it passed. This frightened the woman greatly, and, in fear, she went quickly towards her home. The only explanation that she could give of the strange music was that it was fairy-music."

The next tale is as follows:

"Some miners, engaged in opening a work, on the Merionethshire hills built a hut by the works, in which they deposited their tools on finishing the labours of the day, and one of their number slept in this hut. The watcher one night, when seated in the hut enjoying his pipe, heard a tune played on a violin outside. He got up to see who it was who was there, but when he had opened the door the fiddler and the tune had gone a distance off. It was a dark night, and a drizzling rain was falling, and he could not see far because of the rain and mist, but he stood by the door listening, and he heard the music until at last, apparently in consequence of the distance it was from him, he could hear it no more. This man was fully persuaded that no mortal fiddler played that tune."

I have suppressed the names of these tales, at the request of my friend, the Vicar, who does not wish them to appear, neither does he himself, happy man, want to be immortalized by having his name mentioned in these notes.

December 16, 1891 *E.O.*

A Smoke And A Pint

Did Sir Walter Raleigh introduce smoking into England, or did he introduce *tobacco* smoking? There are small pipes called 'Fairy Pipes' often found embedded in the earth and in the ruins of cottagers' abodes. The bowl is just big enough to admit the tip of the little finger, and they seem to be very old. The quantity of smoking stuff they are able to hold is so small that apparently something stronger than tobacco was used.

The other day, when travelling in the train with an intelligent working man, an aged Cheshire man, who was a botanist, I was informed by him that the agricultural labouring men in Cheshire smoke the foliage of the coltsfoot and May-bright as substitutes for tobacco, and he also named some wild plant which they smoked. Does this post-date or ante-date tobacco smoking? We cannot really be positive that these substitutes for tobacco were smoked by the farm labourers from remote times, but taken in conjunction with the fairy pipes, it would seem smoking is an old indulgence in England.

November 27, 1895 *E.O.*

In a recent number of a publication called *Answers* the following paragraph appeared.

"All Welsh counties swear by a drink called 'sow beer'. It is made from 14 different field herbs, is harmless, except for its sleeping effects, and resembles treacle more than anything. The Welsh villagers smoke a thin cigarette of dried sage when they drink sow beer. The stuff is too complicated for the villagers to brew, but in all large towns there are dealers who make it. The whole output is calculated at 80,000 pints already, and the average price runs to 4d a pint."

October 14, 1896   *D.M.R.*

Witchcraft In Evidence

The belief in witchcraft is not yet dead. At Caernarvonshire Petty Sessions, on Saturday, before Captain Wynn Griffith and other magistrates, Margaret Evans, Brynllyfni, Llanllyfni, for whom Mr F. A. Evans appeared, was summoned for threatening Margaret Griffith. The parties are neighbours and quarelled about some hens trespassing in a field. The defendant, it was alleged, went to the complainant with a Bible, and after reading a portion of it went down on her knees and prayed the Lord to remove the lot from the face of the earth.

Captain Wynn Griffith: What does the defendant mean by reading a Bible and praying before the complainant?

The Complainant: I suppose she was "sacrificing" (offrymu) us.

Mr Hugh Roberts (magistrate's clerk): She means that the defendant was witching her.

Mr Evans: Some people think they can "witch" by saying two or three psalms or a few sentences from Holy Writ.

The Complainant said that the defendant said a great many silly things, and muttered curses and swore. A police-constable described the defendant as being the terror of the neighbourhood. Mr C. A. Jones called the defendant, who said it was a sin that the complainant was allowed to live. There was a previous charge against the defendant, who was bound over in £20.

April 25, 1883   *Ed.*

On Thursday, the 25th of March, 1830, an inquiry was held before the magistrates at Llanfyllin, which disclosed facts of a remarkable character. A young farmer was charged with shocking brutality to an old woman. The following was the old woman's statement:

"The defendant came to my house, and prevailed on me against my will to accompany him home, and then made me kneel down before the churn and repeat these words 'The blessing of God be on the milk!' On remonstrating with him he pierced a nail through my hand until the blood flowed."

The poor woman showed her wounded hand. The farmer was asked if he had anything to say for himself, when he replied:

"I could not churn, which happened very often, so I thought it best to get the woman to bless the milk. I do not think it would make anyone worse for repeating before the churn, 'The blessing of God on the milk."

But the magistrates thought differently and informed the farmer that there was no freedom for him or anyone else to draw blood from old women or to take them against their will to bless the milk or the churn, as there was really no power in any sorceress to prevent her neighbour from churning. It was a common belief among the old people that to draw the blood out of a witch would prevent her witching anyone else.

November 21, 1894   *Colleninda*

Looking over a collection of newspaper scraps the other day I came across the report of a remarkable trial which took place at the assizes at Monmouth in April, 1827, which I transcribe.

D.J.

"William Watkins, a respectable farmer, John Prosser, a constable, Thomas Jenkins and Henry Evans, farm servants, were charged with a riot and with assaulting Mary Nicholas.

"Mr Maule said he was truly surprised and sorry to lay a case of this kind before a Jury in this enlightened age. The prosecutrix was an aged female, upwards of 90 years of age, whom the prisoners had most absurdly fancied to be a witch, and the prisoner Watkins having had several of his cattle die suddenly fancied that she had bewitched them. Under this notion the four prisoners came to this unfortunate old woman on the road and dragged her by force to the fold-yard of the prisoner Watkins. By this a great concourse of persons was attracted as the scene of the outrage was only one mile from Abergavenny.

"When they got her there they placed her behind a colt and obliged her to kneel on the ground, and take the animal's tail in her hand and repeat some form of prayer, which was to protect the cattle against her spells. This she did, and the prisoners under the stupid notion that if you draw a witch's blood she cannot hurt you, took a bough of a wild rose out of a hedge and drew this across her arm, so as to make it bleed. They then proceeded to strip the upper part of her person for the purpose of finding a supposed mark where she suckled imps, or some sort of beings out of another world, and when they had cut off some of the unfortunate creature's hair they found a wart, which they said was it.

"Upon this they proposed to duck her; but at the earnest entreation of her daughter they let her go. It was most fortunate for the prisoners that they did not carry out their intention of ducking, as if death had ensued they would have been every one of them most seriously answerable for that offence.

"Mr Russell, for the defendants, said he could not deny the assault, and that he was most surprised to find that so much superstition could exist either in England or Wales. It should, however, be recollected that one of the most eminent judges that ever sat in this country (Sir Matthew Hale) believed in all this absurdity as implicitly as the prisoners did. That the prisoners had acted in the belief that the poor woman was a witch was quite clear, as they drew her blood, which was understood to disarm the

49

power of a witch. They cut off her hair, because it was said a witch's hair would not burn, and the ducking her was not for the purpose of drowning her, but because one of the tests of a witch was that she would float on the water.

"The prisoners had offered every compensation in their power since they had been convinced of the delusion under which they had laboured, but that had not been acceded to by the prosecutors.

"Mr Baron Vaughan said that he thought the riot was not proved, but that beyond all question a most brutal assault had been committed. That the prisoners had acted under a delusion founded on superstition was quite clear; and he regretted that there was anyone in the kingdom who should have been so deploringly ignorant as to have fallen into such an error.

"Verdict: Guilty of assault only.

"Mr Baron Vaughan said that from the extreme singularity of the case, he must take time to consider the sentence."
September 6, 1882

I find the following in the *Liverpool Echo*. "There must be men at the bar who remember an extraordinary exhibition of mingled credulity and heroism in a case heard at the Shropshire Assizes. A little child had to give evidence, but her mother would not let her stand alone in the witness-box. She must be there with the child, lest the evil eye should affect her. To make the matter more extraordinary, the person by whom the malignant influence was supposed to be exerted was dead; the person against whom the child was to give evidence was on trial for murdering her."

September 23, 1908   *W.O.*

New Year Customs

In his 'Popular Antiquities' Brand records the fact that "An orange stuck with cloves appears to have been a New Year's gift." So Ben Jonson, in his 'Christmas Masque' — "He has an orange and a rosemary, but not a clove to stick in it." My object in quoting these references is to draw attention to the fact that a practice somewhat similar in its nature is still observed in some parts of Wales. I write of my own knowledge of Glamorganshire.

Children obtain an apple, stick into it three skewers tripod-wise, and a fourth to serve as a handle; and stud it, not with cloves, but with oats and raisins, whilst the whole is well-powdered with wheaten flour and the prominent parts are touched with gold-leaf, and on the top of the apple are stuck sprigs of box and rosemary, and on the ends of the leaves half-cracked hazel-nuts, so that the shells would clasp the foliage. All this is in preparation of New Year's Day, when the "clennig" was carried round in a solemn function of carol-singing and collection.

February 28, 1894   *B.*

"At Tenby there is a very curious custom carried out on New Year's Day, which, we think, must have descended from the times when, in England, holy water was sprinkled during festivals. As New Year's Day was on a Sunday this year, the sprinkling was put off till the Monday. On this day, early in the morning, a bell is rung every five minutes, and when you ask what it all means, you are told that the 'New Year's Waterers' have come round already. The 'New Year Waterers' were really all the children of the place come round in their best clothes, with a mug, or jug, which was filled with water; in the other hand they held a sprig of box. When they have found a person that wants to be sprinkled, they dip the box into the water, and then let the drops from the box-leaves fall on the person. The children expect half-pence, of course, for their trouble. The people who have been sprinkled are supposed to be 'lucky' during the year."

Little Folks Magazine for July.
July 4, 1888   *Ed.*

In several parts of South Wales it was formerly the custom for children to proceed before the dawn of New Year's Day to a well for a jug of water, with which they sprinkled "New Year's Rain" upon all they met, and the doors of the houses of those not yet abroad, singing, meanwhile, this quaint song:

"Here we bring new water
    From the well so clear,
For to worship God with,
    This happy New Year.
Sing levy dew, sing levy dew,
    The water and the wine;
The seven bright gold wives
And the bugles they do shine.

Sing rain of Fair Maid
  With gold upon her toe —
Open you the west door
  And let the Old Year go.
Sing rain of Fair Maid
  With gold upon her chin —
Open you the east door
  And let the New Year in!"

The pity is that such picturesque practises as these should be rapidly dying.

January 17, 1894   *B.*

When at Glan-y-rafon, Trefeglwys, a year ago, I was informed that it had been the custom there from time immemorial to lay the table in the Library, which had a southern aspect, on the morning of the thirteenth of January (Hen Galan) in honour of the reappearance of the sun. The house is situate at the foot of a hill that completely obscures the sun during the depth of winter. I was not informed that any one partook of the repast.

June 26, 1901   *T.H.J.*

An old man, dead for many years, used every New Year's Day to cut a withy stick and put it in his pocket at once, taking the greatest care lest he should let it drop on the ground and then break the charm. I believe he carried it around with him all the year round.

May 10, 1911   *L.C.O.*

A Welsh Volcano?

The Annual Register for 1773 contains the following letter:

                                                    "Holywell, Flintshire, Feb 2

    "The memory of man cannot recollect such quantities of snow to have fallen in these parts, as last week; my house is three stories high, and I can hardly lay me down in security in my garrett. Men, women, children, and cattle, have found their tombs in the snow.

    "The night before last, Moelfamma (a very high mountain in this neighbourhood) was heard to utter, as it were, deep groans; the adjacent hills trembled from their roots. The noise at eleven o'clock was like the sound of distant thunder, from the rolling of huge stones down a craggy precipice. At twelve there was a loud clap, and the vortex of the hill threw up in the same instance vast bodies of combustible matter; liquid fire rolled among the heaps of ruins; at the close of all, nature seemed to make a grand effort, and rent one side of the mountain, which was solid stone, into an hiatus, whose breadth seems to be about 200 yards; the summit of the hill tumbled into the vast opening; and the top appears level, which before was almost perpendicular.

"All is now hushed; but in the places where the fire melted the snow, the earth throws out the verdure of May. At Ruthin, as two persons were foolishly endeavouring to make their escape from the danger, they were buried in a drift; several made their escape from St Asaph into the sea, and fell victims to their timidity."

July 25, 1877   *G.G.*

A further confirmation of this appears in *The Gentleman's Magazine* for March, 1794, p272, where the following passage occurs:

"At Holywell, Flintshire, a noise resembling distant thunder has several times within these few weeks been heard to issue from Moelfammau, a high mountain in that neighbourhood. About 20 years ago the vortex of the hill threw up vast quantities of combustible matter, and one side of the mountain was formed into an hiatus, whose breadth was about 200 yards. The noises which have lately proceeded from the mountain seem to indicate a similar eruption."

July 8, 1885   *E.W.*

Shelley Shot At

There are some interesting and startling incidents connected with the poet's residence in Wales, recorded in 'Shelley Memorials' (King and Co, 1875). It is there stated that when at Tanyrallt, Tremadoc, he contributed towards the expenses of the embankment at Portmadoc; and that he was obliged to leave Wales through fear of his life, being twice shot at.

The first notice of the assault on Shelley appears in a letter to Mr Hookham [his publisher], in which he says, "I have just escaped an atrocious assassination. Oh, send me £20 if you have it. You will perhaps hear of me no more. Friend Percy Shelley." The next letter, written by Shelley's wife, from 35 Cuffe-street, Stephen's Green, Dublin, and dated March 11, 1813, gives a full account of the affair.

"Mr S. promised you," she says, "a recital of the horrible events that caused us to leave Wales. I have undertaken the task, as I wish to spare him, in the present nervous state of his health, everything that recall to his mind the horrors of that night.

"On Friday, the 26th of February, we retired to bed between ten and eleven o'clock. We had been in bed for about half an hour, when Mr S. heard a noise proceeding from one of the parlours. He immediately went downstairs with two pistols which he had loaded that night expecting to have occasion of them. He went into the billiard room where he heard footsteps retreating; he followed into another little room which was called an office. He saw there a man in the act of quitting the room through a glass door which opened into the shrubbery. The man then fired at Mr S., which he avoided. Bysshe then fired, but it flashed in the pan. The man then knocked Bysshe down, and they struggled on the ground. Bysshe then fired his second pistol, which, he thought, wounded him in the shoulder, as he uttered a shriek and got up, when he said these words: 'By God, I shall be revenged! I will murder your wife; I shall ravish your sister! By God, I shall be revenged!'

"He then fled, as we were up for the night. Our servants were not gone to bed, but were just going, when this horrible affair happened. This was about eleven o'clock. We all assembled in the parlour; we were assembled for two hours. Mr S. then advised us to retire, thinking it possible he would make a second attack. We left Bysshe and one man servant who had only arrived that day, and who knew nothing of the house, to sit up.

"I had been in bed for three hours, when I heard a pistol go off. I immediately ran downstairs, when I perceived that Bysshe's flannel gown had been shot through, and the window curtain. Bysshe had sent Daniel to see what hour it was, when he heard a noise at the window. He went there, and the man thrust his arm through the glass and fired at him. They found the ball through his gown, and he remained unhurt. Mr S. happened to stand sideways; had he stood fronting, the ball must have killed him. Bysshe fired his pistol, but it would not go off, he then aimed a blow at him with an old sword which we found in the house. The assassin attempted to get the sword from him, and just as he was getting it away, Dan. rushed into the room, when he made his escape. This was at four in the morning. It had been a most dreadful night; the wind was loud as thunder, and rain descended in torrents.

"Nothing has been heard of him; and we have every reason to believe it was no stranger, as there is a man of the name of Leeson, who the next morning that it happened, went and told the shopkeepers of Tremadoc that it was a tale of Mr Shelley's, to impose upon them that he might leave the country without paying his bills. This they believed, and none of them attempted to do anything towards his discovery. This Mr Leeson has been heard to say that he was determined to drive us out of the country. He once happened to get hold of a little pamphlet Shelley had printed in Dublin; this he sent up to Government. In fact, he was forever saying something against us, and that because we were determined not to admit him to our house because we had heard his character, and from many acts of his we find that he was malignant to the greatest degree and cruel."

March 27, 1878 *W.R.H.*

The Flying Man

In the wall near the west door of St Mary's Church [Shrewsbury] is a tablet, bearing the following inscription:

"Let this small monument record the name

Of Cadman, and to future times proclaim,

How by'n attempt to fly from this high spire,

Across the Sabrine stream, he did acquire

His fatal end. 'Twas not for want of skill

Or courage to perform the task he fell:

No, no, a faulty cord being drawn too tight,

Hurried his soul on high to take her flight,

Which bid the body here below, good night."

Feb 2, 1739. Aged 28.

On Candlemas Day, 1739, a man named Robert Cadman attempted to slide down a rope, from St Mary's spire, which is more than 200 feet high. One end was fastened to the window nearest the vane, and the other to a tree in the Gay. The following handbill had been issued:

"That the famous Robert Cadman intends to fly off St Mary's steeple over the River Severn, on Saturday next, flying up and down, firing off two Pistols, and acting several diverting Tricks and Trades upon the Rope, which will be very diverting to the Spectators."

Before beginning the descent, he found the rope was too tight, and gave a signal for it to be slackened, but this was misunderstood by the persons below, who made it tighter still, and as the unfortunate man was passing the Dominican Friary, it snapped, and he fell with great force, near the gateway in St Mary's Water Lane. The weather was very severe at the time, and the ground was frozen, so hard that the body rebounded several feet. Thousands of spectators saw the awful sight, and his wife, who was in the crowd collecting money, threw away her gains and rushed to the spot. Some verses on the event, published in the *Gentleman's Magazine*, February, 1740, relate that:

"The gazing town was shocked at the rebound
Of shattered bone that rattle on the ground;
The broken cord rolls on in various turns,
Smokes in the whirl, and as it runs it burns."

It is said that Cadman was a native of Shrewsbury, but this is not certain, although people of the name have been inhabitants, and one, at least, was a burgess. If the rope had held good it seems not unlikely that he would have accomplished his task, for he had performed many exploits at the top of the spire, and the verses before quoted, say:

"The proudest spire in Salops's lofty town
Safely he gains, and glides as safely down."

The following lines on the subject are from a scarce poem, called 'Shrewsbury Quarry', published in 1770:

"Icarian Cadman next invites the Muse
For who can Cadman's hapless fall refuse;
Ambitious he, for Cadman fain would climb,
The subject sad, the labour of my rhyme;
He felt, like Sweden's Charles, the sudden stroke,
His false security beneath him broke.
In sloping progress made his swift descent,
Too near the water, not the sun he went.
Take them, oh Cadman, take the long farewell;
You rose like Magus, and like Magus, fell;
Lavish of life you fell, and future fame,
Nor left a river, nor a brook your name;
Yet Salop's sons lament your doom with tears,
Your lot remember'd through a length of years;
Your stone inscrib'd with living verse, shall tell
How high, alas! you soar'd, how low you fell;
Let that your manes, Cadman, satisfie;
For that alone you should rejoice to die;
The heart humane can human faults forget,
Your fame and fortitude remember'd yet."

February 25, 1874   *R.E.D.*

57

According to Mr Ireland, the man in Hogarth's celebrated picture of Southwark Fair, "descending from a steeple, is intended to represent one 'Cadman', who in the memory of some persons now living performed the same feat at St Martin's in the Fields, from the steeple of which he descended into the Mews." See Ireland's 'Hogarth', vol 1, p79, second edit., 1793.

December 16, 1874   *Nemo*

Heavy Duty

On Wednesday the body of Mr J. L. Stubbs of Shifnal was interred in the parish cemetery at Shifnal. The funeral attracted much attention, as the deceased was one of the biggest men in the county of Salop, weighing about 3¼ cwt. The coffin (of oak) was 37in. across the shoulders, 7ft long and 2ft deep, and took the united strength of ten men to lift it when the corpse was placed in it. Planks were placed against the bedroom window, and the coffin was lowered onto a railway truck, and was thus wheeled to the churchyard. The ground was cut away at the head of the grave to form an incline and the coffin was allowed to slide into its resting place. A large number of people witnessed the ceremony.

January 16, 1884   *Ed.*

Epitaphs

It is well when walking about a county to pass no churchyard or old chapel burying-ground without scanning its earliest headstones: once and again, one comes across something worthy of preservation. Here let a few be put in the safe custody of print: perchance an as yet unborn parish historian may be glad to have them.

Rock Baptist Chapel Yard

"Here / lyeth the Body / of / ROGER WALKER, late / Minister of ye / Gospel / he dyed, March ye 31st / 1748. Aged 62 /

While on ye Earth I was upon the Rock
I daily strove to Feed my Saviour's flock
& now my lips are clos'd yet ye same Stone
Shall teach us, constant readers every one

Fear God in time, & make his word thy guide
Let Sin be hated, & quite laid aside
Take ye my last advice, live just & true
We soon shall meet in bliss, — till then adue."

Coscob Church Yard
"H.S.I. Hugo Dale, Qui obijt 7 Martij, Ano. 1709; Et AEtatis, 80
Go in why stand
ye Gazing on
The Name That's
carved upon this Stone,
Here lies Hugh Dale
That Honest Man
Tell the Contrary
Tell who Can."

March 13, 1912   *Geo. Eyre Evans*

While on a visit to Llanllugan church recently I read the following lines on a tomb-stone erected "in memory of John Baines, who departed this life Feb 12, 1809, aged 65," which may be of interest to some of your readers:
"Many years I've toil'd and till'd the ground,
But in it now a resting place I've found,
That like the purest wheat may spring from dust,
So I may share the joyful harvest of the just."

July 8, 1903   *Viator*

The following epitaph was copied some years ago from a tombstone in Towyn Churchyard, which had been erected to the memory of a gardener, who for half-a-century had been a faithful servant in the Ynyn-y-maengwyn family:

"If honest labour, industry and truth,
Can claim from righteous heaven a just reward,
Learn, learn, ye Welshmen all, both age and youth,
How poor and patient merit claims regard.
Here lies a man who never swerved at all,
His honest heart was only known to a few,
His honest labour furnish'd means but small,
His worth too little known — his names John Hugh."

August 17, 1904 *G.R.*

The word "shut" in Shropshire, says Mrs E. M. Wright in 'Rustic Speech and Folklore' (Oxford University Press), means to yoke horses to the implements, and the following epitaph, in which "unshut" occurs, is given from a tombstone in Ludlow Churchyard, over the grave of one John Abingdon, "who for forty years drove the Ludlow stage to London, a trusty servant, a careful driver and an honest man:"

"His labour done, no more to town,
His onward course he bends;
His team's unshut, his whip's laid up,
And here his journey ends.
Death locked his wheels and gave him rest,
And never more to move,
Till Christ shall call him with the blest,
To heavenly realms above."

June 24, 1914 *Borderer*

In Aberystwyth Churchyard:

"Here
Lieth the Body of David Davies
Smith Aberystwyth
who departed this life
Dec 21st 1818 aged 91

My Sledge and hammer lies reclined
My Bellows too have lost their wind
My fire extinct, my forge decay
And in the dust my vice is laid,
My coal is spent my iron's done
My nails are drove my life is done."

October 28, 1874   *R.T.*

On an old woman who kept a potter's shop at Chester:
   "Beneath this stone lies old KATHARINE GRAY,
Chang'd from a busy life to lifeless CLAY;
By EARTH and CLAY she got her pelf,
But now is turned to EARTH herself.
Ye weeping friends, let me advise,
Abate your grief, and dry your eyes;
For what avails a flood of tears?
Who knows but in a run of years,
In some tall PITCHER, or broad PAN,
She in her SHOP MAY BE AGAIN?"

July 6, 1898   *Bonwm*

   The following epitaph has come into my possession, and may be
considered good enough for a place in 'BYE-GONES'. I am told the
author had more than a local reputation as a poet:
   "An epitaph composed by the late Rev David Richards, vicar of
Llansilin:
   "Here lieth the body of poor old Nump,
Who lived and died at a venture.
He was a plague to his wife all the days of her life
And to his neighbours a daily tormentor."
The author died about the year 1825.

October 2, 1912   *Silin*

In *Shreds and Patches*, 1875, p150, "J.C.", writing on the Dialect of Shropshire, says: "In reference to the word 'cack', I once heard a good — if a little dirty — application of the word. One evening, some years ago, there were present, among others, Ousley and George Maxon. Ousley had been composing rhyming epitaphs upon the names of several persons. Maxon declared that his name was too difficult for rhyming, when Ousley burst out in his stammering style:

"Beneath this stone lies George Maxon,
A name every little child cacks on."
December 6, 1876   *Spot*

Strange Rain

On Sunday morning, February 22, during a heavy rainstorm at Dinas Mawddwy, the rain was observed to be of a grey muddy colour, something very much like that of the water that flows off a ploughed field. All supplies of rain-water were completely spoiled.

Corr

Between 11 and 12 on Sunday morning there fell in the district and neighbourhood of Nant-mawr, extending for some miles around, a shower of rain, which when collected, had the appearance of lime water. As previous rains had cleansed the roots, the colour cannot be accounted for in this way.

Enquirer

Mr Tatton of the Gardens, Petton, wrties to a contemporary, saying that before dinner time on Sunday all the cisterns and rain tubs were filled with a dirty-looking water, grey coloured, nearly like that which is got out of

62

engine boilers. The rain on the edges of the squares on the conservatory and other houses was just the same, and the rain tubs, a mile away, were full of exactly the same coloured water. The atmosphere was thick, like small rain, in the afternoon, but it was not rain or misty rain. People about Petton think it is due to a volcanic eruption somewhere.

— The same thing was noticed in the Oswestry district. At Maesbury some tanks of rain water that on the Saturday night were quite clear when seen on Sunday morning contained water which was just the colour Mr Tatton describes.

— On Sunday morning, about 10am, a shower of muddy rain fell in Llansantffraid. The water in the bath was like that of a river in flood. The wind was south-west at the time.

A similar statement comes from CLYNDERWEN, near Narberth, Pembrokeshire.

February 25, 1903 *Ed.*

Fortunately, a good sample of the coloured rain which fell on Sunday, February 22, was secured by Mr E. D. Jones, of Meirionfa, Dinas Mawddwy. He has communicated to the Secretary of the Meteorological Society, and I think the reply (enclosed) will be of interest to readers of your science column, especially as to the light which it throws on the possible origin of the dust. Hitherto, the theory held locally has inclined to a volcanic origin, possibly fine ashes from a volcanic outburst in Iceland. Meteoric dust has been suggested. The result of the investigation by the Meteorological Society will be awaited with interest. A sample which I have shows a deposit very much like a fine sand of a brown colour, similar to the sand of the sea shore.

"Meteorological Offices, 63, Victoria-street, S.W.

Sir — I am directed by the Secretary to thank you for your letter of the 25th of February, drawing his attention to the fall of discoloured rain which occurred last Sunday. Similar reports are to hand from a considerable number of places in the South of England and Wales. The Secretary would be grateful to receive a sample of the deposit for a comparison with other samples — the derscriptions given by different observers do not all agree. The samples that I have seen hitherto resemble the dust which fell in Cornwall in January, 1902, which was carefully examined by Dr Mill, who inclined to the view that it was fine sand from the Sahara, carried out to sea in the first instance, and then brought to our shores by a S.W. wind.

— I am, sir, your obedient servant, R. G. K. Lempfert."
March 4, 1903   *Min-y-Llyn*

The enclosed cutting, from the *Daily Express*, gives very substantial support to Dr Mills's theory as to the Sahara being the originating point of the storm of January, 1902. The same evidence may apply to the recent storm. It will be noticed that according to the account given, the storm at sea was observed before and after the date upon which it arrived in this country. The great distance traversed by the storm suggests many interesting reflections:

"The Union Castle Company's steamer Dunolly Castle, bound for London, on touching at Plymouth reported her experiences of the terrific sand storm which she encountered when 200 degs. north of the Equator, and which lasted within about thirty-six hours of her arrival at the Canary Islands. A traveller, who has been voyaging in these latitudes for the last thirty-seven years, informed an *Express* representative that the storm was the worst he had ever known. It was on February 22, that the Dunolly Castle fell in with the storm, the air being charged with sand swept from the Sahara Desert. It was quite as bad as the densest fog. So thick was the atmosphere that it was impossible to see from end to end of the steamer for many hours, and it was found necessary to proceed with the utmost caution. For three days the liner was passing through the storm, which was all the more remarkable as at times the Dunolly Castle was 200 miles from the African shore. The duration of the storm was remarkable. As far back as February 19 the West African mail steamer Bornu fell in with it five days out from Sierra Leone, and for thirty-six hours had to proceed "dead slow". For a time she had for company the large steamer, Springfield, which was wrecked through taking a wrong course in the storm."
March 11, 1903   *Min-y-Llyn*

The inhabitants of Lampeter and district have been startled by some extraordinary rainfall. The showers, which were heavy, came down in unusually large drops, in colour very much like porter. Where quantities were caught in vessels, the water, if such it could be called, appeared as black as ink. Many theories are advanced to explain this remarkable phenomenon; but the one generally accepted is that the showers came from the peat bogs in the south of Ireland opposite this part of the Welsh coastline, or that they were home of the black waters of Stroud. The showers had a singular effect upon the land, making the grass and also ploughed fields quite dark and black in places. Similar showers were reported from Ireland.

May 18, 1887 *Ed.*

At Cardiff, on Friday, it was noticed that after a fall of rain pools of water in the thoroughfares were tinged with red — the effect of what is known as "red rain". In past generations this appearance produced the gravest alarm, a fall of so-called "bloody rain" being regarded as a sure precursor of plague.

May 29, 1889 *Ed.*

In the 'Proceedings' of the Royal Society for June 26, 1661, mention is made of a miraculous fall of wheat in Shropshire (and other counties).

"Arthur Mason, coming out of Shropshire, reports that it has rained the like in many places of that county. God make us thankful (says the writer) for this miraculous blessing."

I take this from *Notes and Queries*, where it is said the Society came to the conclusion that the "wheat" was in fact "ivy berries, dropped by starlings."

March 14, 1894 *W.O.*

An extraordinary event is recorded from Pwllheli. A number of men were working in the early morning at Gimlet Rock, when an immense number of birds, attracted perhaps by the lights, dropped upon them and the shipping and the beach. They found heaps of all sorts of birds lying dead or dying on the ground, whilst as many had dropped into the sea. This was the case for a great distance along the shore; some of the fields immediately adjacent were also strewn with thousands of feathered creatures in a like stricken condition. The birds included starling, blackbirds, thrushes, and robins, and several snipe were also said to be among the victims. The affair has caused quite a stir in the district.

March 30, 1904 *Ed.*

Bull Ghosts

Once upon a time there was a bull that had no skin, but kept up a continual roaring. This animal frequented a bridge at Bagbury, to the grievous detriment of the people living there. It was declared to be possessed of a devil, and to such a pass had things come that seven parsons out of the district were gathered together in the church to "pray the devil down", or try and exorcise the evil one. In the midst of these proceedings Old Nick himself appeared in *propria persona*, and made his entry with such a rush that the church walls were rent asunder, and all the lights were put out, except one candle, which a ready-witted parson hid in his vestments. Thus the meeting broke up in confusion, but the disturbed clerics were not long in arranging a second gathering, and at this they were more successful, and their labours resulted in the unruly spirit being "laid". The legend continues that they buried it under the southern abutment of the bridge over the Camlad in Churchstoke village, where it is supposed to be safely ensconced at present.

July 12, 1893   *J. E. Tomley*

Miss Burne, in her 'Shropshire Folklore', gives various versions of the story given in BYE-GONES. One variant of the story is that the bull, when he was in the church, swelled till he cracked the walls, but they caught him and put him in a snuff box, and then in the water. A ghostly bull is still seen in those parts.

September 2, 1896   *T.*

About fifty years ago the following story was current in the extensive Shropshire parish of Worthen, which, until 1853, included the Montgomeryshire townships of Leighton, Rhos Goch, and Trelystan (pronounced Trelustan). It is so long since the story was told to me, by a native of the district, that I am not quite sure about some of the details.

Anyhow, a ghost, in the shape of a great bull, was so bold that it used to appear in daylight, and became so terrifying that some parsons were fetched to read it down. Attracted by their appearance, the bull followed them, and they retreated towards Trelystan Church. Their reading was so potent that when they arrived there, the bull, which had been dwindling away, had shrunk so much that it could pass inside the door.

By this time candles were needed, and while they were being procured the bull grew bigger and bigger till the walls began to burst. (My informant had seen the cracks). Luckily, the candles arrived in time to save the church. The parsons read on, with might and main, the bull becoming smaller all the while until he was forced into a bottle, which was thrown into the Red Sea.

August 12, 1903   *Bromlow Callow*

Ten years ago the crack in the beam caused by the bull was plainly seen, but in the interval the church [Trelystan] seems to have been "thoroughly restored", and the other day when I again, after long absence, visited the building, I could not find the opening in the woodwork. The various texts, too, formerly displayed about the church, are no longer to be seen; and what was once a very quaint and unusual building has been more or less reduced to an ordinary and commonplace edifice.

September 2, 1903   *M.E.P.*

Exorcist For Hire

The following advertisement, according to the *Sketch*, appeared in 1777:

"Haunted Houses. Whereas there are mansions and castles in England and Wales which have for many years been uninhabited, and are now falling to decay, by their being haunted and visited by evil spirits, or the spirits of those who for unknown reasons are rendered miserable even in the grave, a gentleman, who has made the tour of Europe, of a particular turn of mind and deeply skilled in the abstruse and sacred science of exorcism, hereby offers his assistance to any owner or proprietor of such premises, and undertakes to render the same free from the visitation of such spirits, be their cause what it may, and render them tenantable and useful to the proprietors. Letters addressed to the Rev John Jones, No. 30, St Martin's-lane, duly answered and interview if required.

N.B. — Rooms rendered habitable in six days."

June 12, 1901   *D.M.R.*

Poe Predicted

The following appears in *Notes and Queries* (8th s. v.366):

"POE'S MURDERS IN THE RUE MÔRGUE: The employment of an Ourang-Outang in the committal of these murders has always seemed to me to be one of the most original ideas in fiction with which I am acquainted until now, when I light upon an extract from the *Shrewsbury Chronicle*, tucked away in *Chronicle* columns of the 'Annual Register'.

"Poe's story was published in *Graham's Magazine* for April, 1841. What took place at Shrewsbury occurred in July or August, 1834. At that time certain showmen visited the town with a 'ribbed-faced baboon', which, it was afterwards shrewdly suspected, had been taught to burgle, or, as the *Chronicle* puts it, to 'commit robberies by night, by climbing up places inaccessible to men, and thereby gaining an entrance through the bedroom windows' — precisely the method of procedure adopted by Poe's anthropoid.

"In her bedroom one night a Shrewsbury lady found the creature. She raised an alarm, and the baboon 'instantly attacked her, and with so much fury that the lady's husband, who had come to the rescue, was glad to let it escape by the windows'. The ourang-outang of the Rue Morgue makes a similar though more fatal attack when it is discovered in a lady's bedroom there, and it effects its escape by the same means.

"It is, of course, possible that Poe may never have come across this episode: but it seems something more than probable that he did. Anyhow, the coincidence is singular."

June 13, 1894   *W.T. Walker, Ed.*

Admiral Composure

The late Mr Gwilliam of All Stretton, whose family for many years occupied a farm at the Sted Valletts, near Downton Castle, told me the following anecdote some years ago. In the early part of 1800 Lord Nelson was for a few days guest of Mr Knight at Downton Castle, near Ludlow. Some of the most influential tenants on the estate, desiring to "interview" his lordship, waited upon Mr Knight, asking him to arrange for their "seeing him" (as they put it). Mr Knight, however, in no measured terms, refused their request, and expressed himself annoyed that they should desire him "to make an exhibition of his guest." It appears, however, that by some means or other his lordship had become acquainted with their wish, and unexpectedly appeared in their midst, remarking "Here I am, my men, short of an eye, and an arm, but what is left of me look at as much as you like." Mr Gwilliam said his grandfather formed one of the deputation.

July 19, 1905   *T. Caswell*

Sheridan's Curse

At the Mold clerks and assistants annual dinner last week, how clerks and assistants should improve their position was, of course, elbowed out by the news that the army is now in a transition state, that Englishmen wherever found would do their duty, that the Bishop of St Asaph is a Welsh-speaking prelate, and other like startling information. Mr Ellis Eyton, MP, enlivened the proceedings by quoting, amid great laughter, the following lines from Sheridan, who paid a visit to the town in very wet weather:

"Were I to curse the man I hate,
　From youth till I grow old,
Oh! might he be condemned by fate
　To waste his days in Mold"

That, Mr Eyton added, was not quite applicable to the rising town of Mold.

January 20, 1875   *Ed.*

An Evil Welcome

Nearly two hundred years ago a Welsh Claimant seems to have come to grief not far from Orme's Head. The story is related by Mr Williams in his 'History of Aberconwy', 1835. It relates to an ancient farmhouse on the coast called Penrhyn. The author says:

"At the time of the following occurrence, the family at Penrhyn consisted of a son and two daughters; the former, according to the practice of the age, went on his travels abroad; but before he set out, he took the precaution of putting a needle between one of the joints of the ceiling in the little kitchen, and he also drove the tooth of a harrow into a pear tree in the orchard.

"After a lapse of many years, and all hopes of his return being given over, he arrived a beggar, and coming home he found his parents dead, and his sisters in possession of the property. He stated who he was; but his sisters insisted that he was an imposter, asserting that they were certified of their brother's death: to prove his identity, he said that the needle would be found in a certain place, and as a further proof he named a particular tree into which he had driven the harrow tooth. The needle was found, and when they followed him to the orchard, he removed the bark which had grown over the iron, and shewed it to his sisters; notwithstanding he was forcibly ejected from the premises, and it is said he was flogged with a whip, in which large pins were fixed, as an additional punishment for his supposed imposture.

"He was received into the neighbouring cottage by the inhabitants, who had known him before he went abroad . . . But having gone out one day, he was missed and never returned. . . . The tenants of Penrhyn, not many years since had occasion to build a lime kiln, and in a fissure of the arch immediately behind the house found a skeleton."

March 4, 1874 *Ed*

The Stone Of Contention

In persuing the Llanfyllin parish magazine for the present month I notice the following:

"Tradition asserts that D. Maurice, of Penybont, caused the carregybig, or 'stone of contention', to be removed from the centre of Llanrhaiadr village, in consequence of the great fighting caused by the assumption by the prize-fighter of the neighbourhood of the title of 'captain', by leaping on the stone and proclaiming himself 'Captain Carregybig'. This was carried to such a pitch that the Vicar of Llanrhaiadr begged David Maurice to remove the stone, which he did with a team of oxen, and placed it in his farmyard; when lo! and behold! the cattle, horses, sheep, and pigs, like maddened creatures, danced and pranced about the stone, ending their joust with horning, biting and eventually killing each other at the shrine of the 'stone of contention'. David Maurice, thinking the place haunted because of the stone, caused it to be rolled into the river near at hand, thinking the 'charm would be thereby broken'.

"The Rev Walter Davies, Gwallter Mechain, who is generally considered a very high authority on every branch of Welsh literature and history, has the following remark on the subject in his notes on the works of Huw Morris, vol 2, page 358: 'The affrays here complained of by the Bard, were, in former times, frequent and bloody. A ruffian, in possession of the summit of Carregybig, a large stone then in the town, proclaimed himself its champion. This was to be understood as a general challenge; and it was commonly accepted by an antagonist of supposed equal strength and ferocity. These savage exhibitions continued more or less in practice at fair and wake times, until the 'stone of contention' (carregybig) was removed and deposited in the deepest part of the adjacent river (that means the Rhaiadr and not the Tanat), by the orders of the deservedly respected Dr Worthington, who was collated Vicar of the parish in 1745. The stone, the apparent cause of such frequent pugilistic feats, being thus removed, the effect soon ceased; and peace and good order has been ever since established, upon an equality with other places under the same government'."

Walter Davies was born in the parish of Llanfechain, adjoining Llanrhaiadr, and was seventeen years of age when Dr Worthington died, October 6, 1778, and might have seen the stone at Llanrhaiadr. No doubt the testimony of Gwallter Mechain is conclusive to every unbiased mind in this small matter.

April 15, 1896   *Llywarch Hen*

Wreckers Get Wrecked

The *Universal Magazine* of 1769 contains under date of March 6, this paragraph:

"A person lately arrived in town from South Wales gives the few following particulars consequent of a wreck on the coast of that country. A large vessel, laden with Spanish wine and brandy, having run ashore at Cowbridge, near Cardiff in Glamorganshire, a number of the country people assembled, and in the plunder of the said vessel showed the most savage disposition. They boarded the vessel, and took the greatest part of the cargo out, but were prevented getting the remainder by one of them dropping a lighted candle into a cask of rum, which set fire to the ship, and burnt her to the water's edge. The captain, on his knees, entreated them not to destroy his papers, but such was their inhumanity, that they tore them piece by piece before his face. Thirteen of the passengers drank so immoderately that they died on the spot, and what liquid could not be conveyed away they staved upon the rock. The country about, since the above affair, has exhibited a scene of the greatest rioting and drunkenness."

July 25, 1894   *B.*

Poetic Tax Return

The following curious return was made to the Commissioners of the Income Tax in the year 1801, at Shrewsbury:

"I, A.B. do declare
I have but little money to spare
      I have
1 little house,
1 little maid,
2 little boys,
2 little trade;
2 little land,
2 little money to command.
      By this you see
I have children three,
Depend on me, A.B."

February 17, 1886

Ed.

Nursery Rhymes

The enclosed Nursery and School Rhymes are used in this (Tregynon) district. I am not absolutely certain that they are all complete or correct:

Grandsire Grig
Bought a pig,
And turned him in the clover;
Piggy died,
And Grandsire cried,
And all the fun was over.

Rabbits hot
And rabbits cold,
Rabbits young
And rabbits old.
Rabbits tender
And rabbits tough,
Never can we have enough.

There was a little man
Who had a little gun,
His bullets were made of lead:
He went to the bruck
And shot at a duck,
And hit her upon the head,
                              Dead, dead, dead.

Little Poll Parrot
Sat up in the garrett;
Eating her toast and her tea:
There came a blind spider,
And sat o' one side of her;
And frighten'd poor Polly away.

Three straws in a pie,
Will make a baby laugh and cry.

Little Dio dumpling,
Boil him in the pot;
Sugar him, and butter him,
And eat him while he's hot.

Tripady, trapidy, trauncher,
Carry the lady to launch her,
When you come to London bridge,
Throw her in the water.

See-saw, jackdaw,
The woodcock and the sparrow;
The little dog has burnt his tail,
And shall be hang'd tomorrow.

F for Francis
I for chances
N for Nicholas
I for tickle us
S for Sammy the Saltbox.

Churn butter,
In the gutter;
Wash thy hands, slut.

Black eye, pick a pie,
Stole a goose, and told a lie;
Grey eye, greddy gut,
Swallow all the world up.

The little pig said, I want some red wheat;
And this said, where shall we get it?
The little pig said, in dada's barn;
And this said, there can be no harm;
And this little pig said, wich, wich, wich,
I cannot get over the barn-door sill
Because I am so very ill.

Give a thing,
Take a thing,
Wear the bwgan's ring.

This is used as a retort for taking anything, once given, but strictly speaking it is a relic of witchcraft, a form of "overlooking."

July 16, 1890   *T.H.J.*

The following nursery rhyme was heard by the writer in the parish of Llanbedrog:

1, 2, 3, 4, 5, 6, 7,
All good children go to heaven,
Penny on the water,
Tuppence on the sea,
Threepence on the railway,
Out goes she.

May 20, 1896   *W.A.D.*

A writer in *Notes and Queries* gives the following as a Glamorganshire variant of a nursery rhyme:

My father died a month ago
    And left me all his riches,
A feather bed, and a wooden leg,
    And a pair of leather breeches.

He left me a teapot without a spout,
    A cup without a handle,
A tobacco-pipe without a lid,
    And half a farthing candle.

March 23, 1894   *W.O.*

These were noted down [at Tong] thirty years ago:

    Peg Peg, with a wooden leg, through the field she goes;
With a rick, stick, stack, and a bottle on her back,
                and a pancake tied to her nose.
Billy Button went to Sutton on his little pony,
He stuck a feather in his cap, and called it Macaroni.

Georgie, Porgy, pudding and pie, kissed the girls and made them cry
When the girls came out to play Georgie Porgie ran away.

Charlie, Charlie, chuck, chuck, chuck, went to bed with
                   three young ducks
The youngest died and Charlie cried, Charlie, Charlie,
                 chuck, chuck, chuck.

Hurroo Bob, with a carrotty knob,
    your father was a tinker,
He made your mother a warming pan
    to last her all the winter.

Claydabber Dick, three farthings a week,
For three little urchins to carry one brick.

Sophy, Sophy, the cat's got your bustle on.
December 15, 1915   *John H. Clarke*

Mix Match

Newspapers early in the century had an unpleasant way of noting any peculiarity in connection with courtship and marriage. I have just been running over some lists for 1808. In one we have appended to the announcement, that "the bridegroom crawled to the church on crutches"; in another that the ceremony took place after "a tedious courtship of three weeks."

A third reads as follows (and is from a paper dated June 3, 1808): "Wednesday week, at Welch Hampton, Mr Joshua Lewis, of Breaden Heath to Miss Glover of Ellesmere: the bridegroom is 17 years of age and the bride 83; — just a century between them!"
June 3, 1885   *Scrobbes Byrig*

The following is from the *Worcester Herald*, and extracted from its issue of July 8, 1707: "Married. — Lately, Mr Laley, of Acton, in Cheshire, aged 74, to Miss Coffin, of Whitchurch, Shropshire, aged 23. Seventy-four and a coffin cannot be an ill-timed match."
August 4, 1897   *P.O.A.*

From *Observer* of Sunday, June 28th, 1801: "Remarkable Marriage. At Wentnor, Salop, Richard Finch, aged 17, to Mrs Ann Wigley, aged 89."
March 19, 1902   *T.R.H.*

The following extract from an old magazine (1768-70) may interest some readers of BYE-GONES: "1768: 5th Jan: A maiden lady, possessed of considerable estate in Shropshire, aged 63, to her steward's son, aged 19."
December 6, 1905   *T. Caswell*

St Mark's Eve

The following are Border versions of the superstitions attached to St Mark's Eve [April 26]:

Take a walk between 11 and 12 o'clock at night in the churchyard and sit on twelve gravestones for five minutes on each, except that on the last (it should, if possible, be right opposite the church porch door) you must only sit four minutes, so as to be at the porch door as the clock strikes 12; on the first stroke you will see a man go in church. Stand in the same place and wait until the clock finishes striking, and when it strikes the last stroke and you see the man come out, either you or one of your relations will be married before another St Mark's Eve; but if the man does not come out, either you or one of your relations will be dead before another St Mark's Eve. You should go in the churchyard as the clock strikes 11 pm.

If you and another lady friend should be sitting in the house you must lay the supper cloth for four, but if you should happen to be alone lay for two, putting on the table six glass tumblers upside down, and two knives to each, and sit down with every door of the house open, and wait until the clock strikes 12, and then you will see either four or two young men come in, according to how many you have laid supper for, and if they take hold of one of the tumblers and put it to your eyes, in the course of a year you will be nearly blind and can only see with the aid of spectacles, but if they take hold of one of the knives by the blade and hold it to your face and laugh, they will be the cause of your death with the same knife that day twelve months.

Go up into your bedroom, the room being in total darkness, and stand before your looking-glass as the clock strikes 11, with the glass upside-down, and just as it is on the stroke of 12 turn the glass up and look for one instant. You will see a figure. If you cannot see it very clearly there is trouble for you and the figure is an enemy, but if you can see it clearly enough to scan its features it is a friend, and you will have plenty and prosper in your business. Then as the clock is striking the hour go on your bed, and lie flat on your back, and stare at the ceiling, and if the same figure, whichever of the two, comes round your bed three times, it is a sign you will have three attacks from the enemy or three visits from the friend, but you must not let your face bear the least trace of a smile, but look very sorrowful.

Go into your garden at a quarter to 12 pm, and walk three times round it. After you have made the third round, stand still and keep your eyes fixed on the roof of your house. While standing, keep your hand, if possible, on a fruit bush of any kind (but it must not be a tree), and listen, as the clock strikes 12, whether there is the slightest noise. Do not turn your eyes from the roof. Then if the slates of the top of the house raise themselves up and go flat down into their proper places again, you will have very bad news of a friend or a relative, informing you either of their death or illness. If the slates rise up and fall down close to where you are, it is a sign your death will be caused either by something heavy falling down from a great height upon you, or by your falling from a great height; but, whichever you see, if the bushes prick your hands, or you happen to see a light shining somewhere, it is a sign you will be warned of your danger before it be too late. All must be done before the clock stops striking, or as it finishes striking the hour of 12.

(We give these superstitions just as they were written by a servant maid belonging to Oswestry. — Ed.)

June 18 and 25, 1890   *A.*

Easter Customs

In Carnarvon it was the custom for children to go about at Eastertide with a wooden clapper begging for eggs, and crying the while —

"Clap, clap, ŵy pasc
Os gwelwch chwi'n dda, ga'i ŵy."
"Clap, clap, easter egg,
Please give me an egg."

They seldom failed in getting their request. In the west part of Denbighshire a like custom prevailed. The custom was once general in North Wales. At Easter time — on Easter Sunday — servants now have an egg with their breakfast. This is the case in Denbighshire.

It was formerly the custom for clergy to get eggs from the parishioners at Easter. This became a due, and is mentioned in many terriers. Thus in Cerrigydrudion Terrier, 1749, is the following entry: "Tyth eggs, two for every cock, and one for every hen in the parish, this kind of Tyth is gathered every year a little before Easter. In Llanyckil (Llanycil, Bala) terrier under the year 1774 is the entry: "Of eggs two for every cock and one for every hen." Other quotations need not be given.

Even after tithes were commuted, the farmer's wife in many parishes sent a present of eggs to the clergyman. This has not entirely ceased in our days. A person who gave evidence at Llangollen before the Welsh Land Commission stated that: "The parish clerk or his servant used to go round and count the hens, and the farmer had to give an egg for each hen and two for each cock." He did not state how long ago this was. This is a pity, for had he done so, we should have known when the small tithe ceased to be collected. He merely mentioned the fact as a grievance, suffered possibly by his grandfather, which he resented. He evidently did not understand the meaning of this kind of offering. As to the origin of the custom, I cannot dare to say anything, excepting that it is probable we should have to go outside Wales for it, and possibly we shall have to travel back for long years, before we arrive at its beginning.

August 21, 1895   *E.O.*

One of the Border customs at Easter was that every dish prepared for Easter Sunday should have eggs as the principal ingredient, and in every household a "yellow" cake was made, a sort of seed cake, something similar to Cornish saffron cake. Eggs were eaten at every meal.

March 31, 1897   *AC-H*

In Loveday's 'Diary of a Tour in 1732' (p.25), I find "They have a custom at Bangor and at Caernarvon, too, on an Easter and Whit-Monday, on May-day &c for y'e young fellows y'can get up soon in y'e morning to

79

come and pull y'ir comrades out of bed, put them in y'e stocks & holding
up one of y'ir legs, pour a pail of water down it."

November 4, 1896   *N.W.T.*

An account of an old Easter Sunday custom at Conway was contributed to
the *Cambrian Quarterly Magazine* (vol iii p366) by one Caradawg, and
dated Rhydychen, Mai 16, 1831. The proceedings begin with a
proclamation by the man last married, or, if he could not be found, his
predecessor.

"When the proclaimer was found, he would march at the head of a large
procession, who bore sticks of gorse, and proceeded from Porthisav,
through Porthyraden, to the hill of Pentwtil. On their arrival at the usual
spot, the crier mounted a little heap of stones collected for the purpose,
and announced that all men under sixty years of age were to appear in the
street before six o'clock on the following morning, and all under forty-five
before four, and all under twenty not to go to bed at all, under penalty of
being put in the stocks; after proclaiming these, and similar notices, loud
cheers were given, and the audience separated: the younger part to form
plans for their amusement during the night, for they never transgressed
by going to bed, and those who owned carts or other such vehicles, to
secure them with chains and locks, as they well knew that they would be in
requisition on the following day.

"Very early on the morrow, the stocks were placed at the bottom of the
street, and a party headed by fifes and drums drew a cart or post-chaise for
the purpose of conveying delinquents to the place of punishment. Having
secured to any house where any unmarried man who ought to have been
up was sleeping, they marched to the stocks, where the proper officer,
having secured his feet, gave a lecture upon idleness and breaking an old
law; then taking hold of his right hand, he asked him a few questions, such
as these: Whether he liked better, the mistress or the maid, ale or
buttermilk; whether he would go through the gate of a field, if open, or
over the stile, etc. If, in his answers, he fixed upon what was obviously
preferable, his hand was the more thickly covered with some dirty mud,
and then he was released with cheers. The sufferer then invariably joined
in the search after others, who underwent the same course.

"About six the servant girls might be seen coming out of their houses,
to satisfy their curiosity, which was punished in the following, singular
manner: they suddenly found one of their shoes snatched from their feet
by one of the gwŷr ieuangc and it cost them a trifling douceur to have it

restored, amounting at most to sixpence, or sometimes only a kiss. The sport generally ended at eight, and they went to seek their breakfasts, after which they met at the Castle, where they spent this and the following day, which are always holidays in those parts, in playing at ball."

April 26, 1905   *Brythonydd*

At Whitchurch, near Cardiff, about a century ago, and for time immemorial previously to that period (says an old writer), it was usual for every married woman, who had never been blessed with issue, to repair to the church-yard on Easter-Monday, being first provided with two dozen tennis balls, one dozen of which were covered with white, and the other dozen with black leather; and these were cast by the fair votaress over the church, from the back-ground, and scrambled for by the populace, who assembled for that purpose in front of the building. So imperative was this custom, that neither rank nor age were excused, until they were relieved, by the birth of a child, from its annual performance.

October 19, 1892   *B.*

Des. Res.

A week or so ago a funeral took place in Condover churchyard, a few miles from Shrewsbury, and a number of wreaths with cards attached were placed upon the grave. One of these was placed there by Mr W. Bratton, teacher of music, who a day or two afterwards again visited the grave, when he found the wreath there, but the card and eighteen inches of ribbon which were attached to it were missing.

It now appears that the thief was "a storm cock", the object of the larceny being the construction of a nest, for the nest has been secured with the ribbon neatly placed inside and the card outside. How the bird undid the knot, which, I am assured, attached the ribbon to the wreath, is an unexplained puzzle.

May 11, 1892   E.

A pair of robins selected a rather curious place to hatch their young this season, the lever of the water closet at the residence of Mr R. Phennah, in Chester-road, Wrexham. The nest is there now, and full of young birds.

May 15, 1895   Ed.

A bird has built a nest at Overton in a pair of old trousers, which are being used as a scarecrow.

May 5, 1897   Ed.

I discovered a wag-tail's nest under the rails at Marchwiel station over which all trains between Wrexham and Ellesmere pass. The nest contained young ones.

June 19, 1901   John Jarvis

A very curious and interesting present has been made to Chester Grosvenor Museum. A sparrowhawk was shot by the head gamekeeper on the Carden Park estate, Cheshire, and hung upon a tree as a scarecrow. Subsequently a keeper discovered that a wren had most ingeniously built its nest upon the bird. The nest is to be seen fixed between the legs and wings of the hawk, on the underside of the body. The head keeper made a present of the hawk and nest to Mr Hart Davies of Chester, who has handed it over to the local museum collection.

June 29, 1898   Ed.

Mr R. W. H. Hodges sends us an account of a Wren's nest in a curious position. A larch tree near Ellesmere has been used by a keeper to nail up his victims. On it are suspended a Carrion Crow, Jay, Sparrow-hawk, Stoat, and several Magpies. The Wren has built its nest between the trunk of the tree and the body of the crow; the nest is half-covered by one of the crow's wings, whilst its feet are woven into the structure so as to support it. There are now young wrens in the nest.

June 14, 1905   *Ed.*

Our Rossett correspondent writes: A most remarkable freak of a starling occurred a short time ago. It flew through an open bedroom window and into the bed, and when the lady of the house went upstairs it was disturbed and flew out. To her astonishment, the starling had laid an egg in the bed.

October 8, 1902   *Ed.*

Avalanche!

I heard my grandmother relating the following in connection with the avalanche about 1809 at Llandrillo. Her father and mother and family had retired for the night, and on awakening in the morning and looking out through the window, were utterly bewildered, not knowing the locality they were in, and after looking around and finding the dwelling house and outbuildings to be the same, they came to the conclusion that the fairies had carried their house to some strange place.

On the neighbours from Llandrillo arriving, they found that an avalanche had taken the whole buildings and carried them down the slope of the mountain until they rested upon a flat surface, and with great difficulty they were rescued from their perilous position, not one having been disturbed in the night, the avalanche having surrounded the buildings and carried them safely down. My grandmother's maiden name was Ffoulkes of Llandrillo.

April 3, 1895   *R.R.*

CURIOUS CASE AT SHROPSHIRE QUARTER SESSIONS — Amongst the records of Coroners' inquisitions in 1772 [is] the following —

"4 women and 3 men who were killed by an inundation of snow out of a dingle, which destroyed their houses, and they were suffocated and smothered, Norbury."

July 27, 1904   *Ed.*

In connection with the foregoing, the following facts may prove not uninteresting to many readers of BYE-GONES. The particulars I gleaned some years back from trustworthy persons residing in the neighbourhood of Wentnor. In Wentnor churchyard is a memorial stone, known as "The Hurricane Stone", bearing the following inscription:

"In Memory of Samuel Perkins, and Mary his wife, and Samuel his son, died February 2nd, 1772, his age 55, his wife 50, his son 15.

On Sunday morn 'Bout Nine o'Clock
As we lay in our Bed,
By Hurricane of Wind and Snow,
All three were Killed dead,
The House and we were Blown away
As many well did know,
And for that day could not be found,
All for the depth of Snow,
Fouteen poor souls were under it,
Out of which were Killed seven,
I hope the lord hath pardoned us
And Received our Souls in Heaven."

Tradition has preserved the following facts: In many country villages, and particularly in secluded and outlying hamlets, it was customary to hold what were called "cakings", the arrangements being that some cottager would brew or buy a barrel of ale and provide "cakes" sufficient for a night's carouse, to which any person, by paying for entrance, was entitled to share. One of the chief attractions was playing games at cards for sundry couples of fowls, for which it frequently happened some adjoining farmer's hen-roost had been "requisitioned". These "cakings" were, to my knowledge, very popular, until within the last forty years, since when, owing a great measure to the county police force, they have become things of the past.

It was upon such an occasion that the "fourteen poor souls", as quoted in the epitaph, were assembled in the cottage of Samuel Perkins, at Asterton, near Wentnor. The house, I am informed, stood on the site where a brick cottage now stands, near Asterton Chapel, at the turn of the road leading to Plowden. Standing in this spot, and looking in a direct line to the side of the Longmynd there are distinct traces of the land-slip from the mountain side, plainly indicating the probability that it was not only a "hurricane of wind and snow", that overwhelmed Perkins's and its unfortunate occupants, but a veritable avalanche of earth and snow. I am informed that four of the victims of the Asterton disaster were buried at Norbury, but I fail to find any memorial in the churchyard there recording the fact.

A similar "slip" from the side of the Longmynd took place at a later date, during a snow storm, when the cottage of a man named Poppett, situate higher up the hillside than that of Perkins, was carried bodily away clear across the road during the night time. A boy going to his work the following morning was the first to make the discovery and give an alarm, saying: "Poppett's house 'as come down the hill and the chimney is poking through the snow." In this instance, Poppett, his wife and his child perished.

July 10, 1904 *Thos. Caswell*

The Electric Whirlwind

The following appears among the extracts from old numbers of the paper which are now appearing in the *Worcester Herald*. The date of the paper is July 8, 1848:

"The following very extraordinary phenomenon occurred on Sunday, the 1st inst., at Lockley Wood, in the parish of Hinstock, near Market Drayton, Shropshire. About nine o'clock in the morning an explosion of the electric fluid burst forth out of the earth with a horrid noise, so as to be heard many miles. In the direction it pursued from the spot where the eruption took place, it acted with all the violence of a tornado; tearing up several trees by the roots, breaking the roots or branches of others, and stripping several cottages &c of their thatch. Two young men who were passing along within the sphere of its activity, were suddenly whirled into the air, and carried into the adjoining fields. The devastation was visible for several miles, but confined to about one hundred yards in breadth."

August 17, 1898 *Ed.*

The Gunpowder Tragedy

The following somewhat singular, and exceedingly frightful, accident took place in Chester on the 5th of Nov. 1772. The writer, communicating the particulars to the papers on the following day, says:

"Yesterday being the anniversary commemoration of the gunpowder-plot, a great number of people of both sexes; men, women and children, went in the evening to see the George Williams's puppet show exhibited at a place called Eaton's dancing hall in Water-gate street; it unfortunately happened, that a neighbouring grocer, had within a few days before, lodged a quantity of gun-powder in a cellar under the showroom, which proved the cause of the most dreadful catastrophe ever known in these parts: for between eight and nine o'clock the powder took fire (how, or by what accident is as yet to be ascertained) and blew up the floor, a room over it, and the roof; shattered the walls, which were of stone, and amazingly thick, and communicating with the scenes, cloths &c., instantly set the whole room in a blaze.

"Thus in a moment were a major part of the company buried under massy ruins, surrounded with flames, without any means of extricating themselves; so that (beside those who were burnt to death, or killed upon the spot by the fall of heavy stones and timber) scarce one escaped, without being so miserably scorched or crushed, that few can survive. The explosion was very great, and attended with a convulsion which was felt in the extremity of the city and the suburbs.

"This alarming circumstance incited many people with a curiosity of inquiring into the cause; which, when known, it is impossible to express the dread with which every one was possessed with for the safety of their family and friends. But when the dead and wounded were seen borne upon men's shoulders along the streets, the scene became affectingly deplorable. Some fainting away, others crying in the bitterest anguish, distracted with the loss of wives, husbands, children and relations; in short the general horror and confusion on this melancholy occasion, is much easier to be imagined than described.

"Among the former are Williams, the showman, his wife, and a child about four years old. The numbers of the wounded are, by later accounts, increased to sixty-six. Much damage is likewise done to the adjacent buildings; several houses being overthrown, and windows shattered to pieces at an incredible distance by the explosion."

The foregoing is taken from the 'Annual Register' for 1772.

November 6, 1878

Nemo

Grannies Bashing

Among 'Leaves From Our Early Issues', *North Wales Chronicle* (March 22 to April 12, 1810), is the following:

"The following singular contest occurred last week at Lampeter in Cardiganshire. Two female paupers, the one 86, the other 88 years of age, who had lived in habits of intimacy, differed about the loss of some yarn, which the younger charged the elder with stealing from her. From words the two matrons proceeded to blows, but the pugilistic encounter terminated without either being vanquished.

"They then agreed to try their skill and strength with cudgels, on Monday the 12th inst., and the bellman proclaimed the combat through the town. After nearly an hour's hard fighting, the younger heroine seemed to have the advantage; and if the civil power had not opportunely interfered would most certainly have killed her antagonist, who, nevertheless, exultingly declared herself one of the 'Cochiel Pencarreg', a name given to a peculiarly obstinate race of fighters, who never call for quarter."

June 18, 1884   *Ed.*

"The Wolf"

Amongst the many mythical diseases created by the superstitious mind, the most to be feared of all was "The Wolf". Women only were subject to this horrible affliction. The wolf is an ailment which only attacks the breast of a woman, and is said to be a living creature, much resembling the head and form of the lizard. The woman so afflicted is said to have in the first instance "taken the wolf" by drinking impure water, and that in time as it further developed itself, it lodged in the breast, where it made a hole, out of which it protruded its head to the great horror of those who could get sight of it. If its hunger were not satisfied with the best of food, most especially roast meats (which it could easily distinguish), its contortions and protrusion of the head were almost unbearable to the afflicted person.

The woman thus troubled — generally a poor beggar — managed the wolf, very much of her own profit, by imposing on the superstitious belief of her well-to-do and charitably disposed neighbours, for if by accident the woman came to a house where there was "the smell of roast meat" she soon made it manifest "how the wolf tore at her breast", and until she was

87

well supplied with the coveted meat "to feed the wolf", her agony continued.

Not many years ago a "wolf" was exhibited by a vendor of medicine on the Bailey Head, Oswestry, safely bottled in spirits and held up as occular testimony of the value of the medicine to the no small wonder of the credulous customers! The last case the writer heard of was near Oswestry.
February 2, 1876   *Gypt*

The Burning Well

The *Gents. Mag* of 1755 contains a letter signed G. Perry, bearing date June 25, containing an account of a Burning Well discovered forty years earlier, "Sixty yards from the River Severn, in the parish of Broseley, at the foot of a gently rising hill, encompas'd on every side with coalworks, though none very near it."

The writer says this was discovered in 1711 by a poor man, who, being alarmed by a very unusual noise in the night, got up and made an examination. "After digging a little, the water gushed out with violence, and took fire at his candle." The man seems to have had his wits about him for he managed to "inclose it with a frame and door, leaving a hole to collect the flame," and thus he contrived to make money by the exhibition, which lasted for some years, until the inflammable matter became exhausted. But in 1747 the man again received warning of the approach of the profitable vapour, at a point ten yards from the old tap, and Mr Perry wrote an account of it to a Birmingham paper. A Cambridge professor (Mr Mason F.R.S.) "inserted a little memoir in the Philos. Trans. on the subject", and the spot became attractive to visitors far and near.

We are told that the water through which this vapour passed never became hot, and when a gentleman commenced digging a coalpit near the place "the undertaking proved expensive and hazardous, the workmen being greatly annoyed by wildfire, and when they had sank it to the depth of 88 yards, and began to get coals, a subterraneous reservoir of brine burst into their works and filled it to a level of 18 yards." The sulphur was so strong after they drained the pit that they determined to fire it, "which caused so terrible an explosion as alarmed all the neighbourhood, imagining it had been an earthquake. It shook their windows, pewter, and even the casks in their cellars. This, however, seemed like a dying groan of the burning well, which since that time has entirely ceased to burn."

We make better use of these "vapours" now-a-days!

June 9, 1875 *Scrobbes Byrig*

Phantom Horsemen

There was an old Welsh tradition in vogue some fifty years ago, that one David Salisbury, son to Harri Goch of Llanrhaiadr near Denbigh and grandson to Thomas Salusbury hen of Lleweni, had given considerable trouble to the living, long after his remains had been laid in the grave. A good old soul, Mr Griffith, of Llandegla, averred that he had seen his ghost, mounted on a white horse, galloping over hedge and ditches in the dead of night, and had heard his "terrible groans" which he concluded proceeded from the weight of sin troubling the unhappy soul, which had to undergo these untimely and unpleasant antics. An old Welsh ballad entitled 'Yspryd Dafydd Salbri' professed to give the true account of the individual in question, but the careful search of many years has failed in securing me a copy of that horrible song.

May 9, 1877 *Goronwy Ifan*

Quite recently a clergyman, well acquainted with the Montgomeryshire of forty years ago, asked if I had ever heard of the phantom horseman, which was supposed to frequent one of the roads leading out of Welshpool? He said that one of the rural mail drivers had been so frightened by it one winter's morning that he had turned back and could not be persuaded to proceed with the bags to some of the neighbouring villages. He said the horseman rode by his side without uttering a word, coming without a sound, and leaving as mysteriously as he had appeared.

July 3, 1901 *Cyffin*

Some years ago I heard the story related by CYFFIN about the ghost who frightened the Wrexham mail-driver on the road between Welshpool and Cann Office. The "event" occurred within the last twenty-five years. The ghost in question is supposed to have been the notorious Yspryd Melin-y-grug, a well-known character in the folklore of Caereinion. The following extract from the late Edward Pentyrch Gittins's entertaining 'History of Llanfair Caereinion' concerning the spirit may be of some interest to the students of Welsh folklore:

"Yspryd Melin-y-grug — This was a ghost appearing after the fashion of a man, riding on a grey or white horse, crossing and re-crossing the road through the hedge. There was a clanging, dismal sound of a chain always to be heard with it. It was supposed to be the spirit of a departed person, with his prison chains on, having permission to visit the old country, and having a warning mesage to bear; but this was never told, because, appearing in a form that was frightening, no one would approach to ask for it. It was the most troublesome spirit of the lot, and caused greatest fright amongst the people."

July 17, 1901   *Cynvelin*

I have more than once been told the story of a phantom horseman that is said to appear at night time near a bridge which spans the river Mule and the railway between Abermule and Fronfraith Mill, on the picturesque Kerry line, and known as the "Captain's Bridge". I do not remember all the details of the story; but the rider is, I believe, connected with some tragic incident which is said to have happened to a gentleman who once lived near, and from whom, I think, the bridge gets its name.

One old person whom I knew would relate, with a certainty that it was difficult to disbelieve, how on one occasion, when she was walking near the bridge, the mysterious white horse and rider dashed by. That she saw them the woman had no manner of doubt, as she told of how she felt the rush of wind as the pair swept past. There was no noise, and horse and

rider disappeared as mysteriously, as they came. There are people now living in that district who firmly believe in the appearance of this phantom horseman.

Mr Horton of Harley Tower, Much Wenlock, tells me a similar story in connection with Harley parish. Some five years ago a farmer set out at dawn with a horse for the Shrewsbury auction. He was passing the Sandy Lane, Harley, when a man on a well-appointed horse passed him, and then mysteriously disappeared. It was so passing strange that the farmer made enquiries, and Mr Horton was told by one old inhabitant that the appearances of this phantom rider are quite well known.

The tradition is that one morning a man was found dead at that place, and his horse near by. The man was said to have come from the neighbourhood of Oswestry, while his dress and the equipment of his horse betokened that he was above the yeoman class. By the body was a note, on which were the words "Between the stirrup and the ground, great mercy I have found." This man now, so some of the people there aver, makes periodical mysterious appearances, while the farmer I mention is emphatic about the excellent saddle and other equipment of the horse that he saw. In both these cases the circumstances are much the same as in that related by CYFFIN, the horseman coming up without uttering a word, passing by without a sound, and disappearing as mysteriously as they came.

July 31, 1901   *W.M.*

In *Household Words* on p1063, of July, is the following:

"In Wales there yet linger many weird, yet fascinating stories of ghosts and fairies. The white horse of Llangynwyd (Glamorganshire) is still believed to haunt the neighbourhood from which it takes its name, and two men at different times have been considerably terrified by an encounter with this snow-white equine spectre. A butcher when riding on horseback one evening saw it looking at him over a gate near Cwmcorion. He did not wait to make investigation, but galloped homewards as fast as his frightened steed would go. Another man was driving through a lane near Llangynwyd on a moonlight night, when suddenly a milk-white horse appeared before him. The animal he was driving reared and snorted with fright, and the driver broke out into cold perspiration. Then the milk-white horse turned and after galloping some distance up the stony lane without making the slightest sound, took a high leap over the hedge and vanished."

August 16, 1905   *J.E.A.*

Following up the local ghost stories you have been publishing, I may give one which I heard many years ago from an aged relative, and a very interesting one it is. In the days long before Llan-y-mynech bridge over the Virniew was built there was somewhere in its neighbourhood a ford, and the road beyond the river was lined on each side by a wood, making it after dark a gloomy spot. This part of the road was said to be haunted by a white horse bridled and saddled, but riderless, which galloped furiously along the dark road from the ford, and upon its shoulders it bore great blood clots.

In her early youth my relative went on Wednesdays to Oswestry market to make the usual purchases, and rode rather a spirited young horse, with a pannier upon the off-side. Upon one particular Wednesday she was much delayed, having more purchases to make than usual, and she returned loaded, the pannier being full, and carried besides over her left arm a bag. She was most anxious to cross over the ford on her return before dark, being made timid by the stories he had heard, but night had set on before she came to it. Loaded as she was, she dreaded the crossing, and it was with difficulty she got her steed to enter the water, but when she had crossed, the spirited animal, smelling his stable, set off at a sharp canter.

While she was incommoded by her load and the pulling of the horse, she distinctly heard behind her the terrifying sound of furious galloping, and her steed, appearing to hear it also, set off furiously in the pitch darkness, and to her horror, glancing behind, she saw coming on at her flank the outstretched head and neck of the white horse. She was now near the end of the wood, and as she emerged the sound of the spectre ceased, but her own animal raced on, only stopping at the gate of the farm, and backing to permit her to fling it open, and then raced for home, where he stood in the farm yard trembling with fear. The family had gone to bed, and only a man was up to attend to the horse, but in the morning she had a sound rating for riding so hard.

May 20, 1903 *M.A.P.*

Dragons

I suppose there are or have been plenty of stories of flying serpents in Wales. There was lately such a tale localised in N.W. Breconshire, in the district N. of Garth Station, where a late and very well known native told my informant of a sarph adenog tanllyd (those were the words used) that flew over from Radnorshire (the boundary of which, the Wye, is only about four miles off), and took up its abode close to a farm called Tan yr Allt, on the banks of the Dulas, whence it committed various ravages (the exact nature of which I now forget) on the surrounding country. In the adjacent part of Radnorshire there is a Carreg Wiber ("the Viper's Rock") near Llandrindod, which was perhaps connected with the same legend.

The word sarph "a serpent" occurs now in a few Welsh place-names, such as Sarffle in Llanarmon Dyffryn Ceiriog, Gwely Sarph near Peniarth, and Sarff-fryn or Sarffryn in Radnorshire, mentioned among the possessions of the Abbey of Cwm Hir in Dugdale's 'Monasticon' (1825) in the form of Sarfbrin.

July 6, 1892 *Egerton Phillimore*

I have been informed that some 50 years ago at Ystradgynlais it was generally believed there was a flying serpent existing on a spot called "Winllan"; it was a rough stony piece of ground covered with brambles on the river side, and is now the site of Yniscedwin Board Schools. Lizards infested the place. My informant suggests that the story was invented to keep children from going blackberrying.

June 10, 1896 *N.W.T.*

CARROG — There was some correspondence respecting this word in the 'Amser Gynt' column of *Goleuad* during the year 1877. One correspondent having referred to a place he spelt Bryncarreg, 'Cynwy' corrects him, and gives a wonderful tradition, connecting the origins of the names of several places in the vicinity of the Conwy with Saint Beuno, and the wonderful creature called Carrog, to the following effect:

"The carrog somewhat resembled a flying serpent. According to popular tradition, this fearful creature sheltered at night in the brushwood that then grew on Dol-y-garrog, and during the day frequently visited Eglwysfach, kidnapping and eating children; and in order to slay this creature Saint Beuno paid a visit to the place, and stayed a few hours at Hafodunos, hence the name (a night's shelter), starting from there soon after midnight that he might reach Eglwysfach at day-break, but he had delayed too long, the dawn was peeping immediately he crossed the Llangerniew mountain, and commenced the descent to Eglwysfach parish; hence the name Ciltwllan.

"It was broad daylight by the time he reached the well, two miles further, which he called Ffynnon Oleu Ddydd (Broad Daylight Well); but after all he reached Eglwysfach very early. He went to the church, and repeated his prayers, and after the sun had shone for some time the Carrog came and lay down on the hill. Saint Beuno ascended the church tower, and directed an arrow from his bow to the tender spot on his throat, which took fatal effect; and it was said this was the only penetrable part of the creature's hide, being like that of a crocodile. Such was the tale that I heard from the old people."

This tale must, of course, be swallowed with a large grain of salt, but I think we may safely conclude that the carrog was a monster, of a species of animal long extinct in Wales.

June 24, 1896   *T.H.J.*

CARROG — It is rather the proper name of a monstrous wild boar which, in Welsh legend, played the part of a medieval dragon in the district of Nant Conwy, NW. At Eglwys Fach, in Denbighshire, there is a tumulus called Bedd Carawg; and tradition says it is the grave of a huge wild boar, killed by Bach ab Carwedd, on the river Carawg. But though he was killed by Bach ab Carwedd, or, according to another version, by the united action of its inhabitants, the boar, as in the case of Diarmait in the Irish story, proved the cause of Bach's death.

December 9, 1896   *G.H.*

Wart Charming

One of our Oswestry elders the other day told me that there were several well-known remedies for warts, which he had tried and proved over and over again.

"When I was a boy", he said, "when any one had warts on his hands we used to get as many grains of wheat as there were warts, and put one on each, and then the grains were tied up in paper, and the person who had the warts went to the nearest crossroads and threw the wheat over his shoulder: and it was thought that whoever picked the parcel up would have the warts, at anyrate they disappeared."

Another remedy he had tried in late years, in the following case: "My grand-son", he said, "had a large wart on his wrist, and one day when we were out I got a snail and touched the wart with it, and then stuck the snail on a thorn, and the wart went away. You may laugh at it", he continued, "but you cannot explain it." I asked him in what space of time the warts disappeared, to which he replied, "Oh, sometimes sooner and sometimes later", and this perhaps may be the explanation.

September 23, 1874   *Jarco*

The following charm for warts was extensively practised at Tong even in recent years. A person having warts would take a bit of white wood, or a piece of peeled stick, and make on it as many notches as he (or she) had warts, then wrap it up in white paper, and place it at some four cross roads, keeping the matter an entire secret from everyone; the warts would be transferred to the finder of the parcel, as they would shortly disappear from the depositor of the charm. However simple and strange the above charm may seem to be, it was certainly believed to be an effective one.

June 28, 1905 *J.H.C.*

About thirty-five years ago, when a boy ten years of age, I had the misfortune of having two big warts right under my foot, which caused me much discomfort, if not pain, in walking. One day, as I was complaining about this to my mother, she advised me to go and see a friend of hers, who was the wife of a prominent man in the neighbourhood. I accordingly went to this lady, who lived close by, and told her everything about the warts.

She directed me to go home and take a small piece of flesh meat and rub the warts with it. Then I was to go out through the back door bearing the flesh with which I had rubbed the warts in one hand, and a spade in the other, and, after proceeding to a field close by, dig a hole in the ground and bury the meat in it and cover it over with earth. She added that during the performance of the ceremony, I was to preserve absolute silence and not to look behind. Moreover, no-one was to know or take notice of what I was about.

As I was only a boy at the time, I did exactly as the woman directed, and, strange to say, within two or three days the warts had entirely disappeared. People believe in, and perform this charm with equal success at the present day in every part of Wales.

January 11, 1905 *Johnathan Ceredig Davies*

I lately met a man who said that he had got rid of many warts by rubbing them with the pod of a bean and then burying the pod in the ground. As the pod decayed, so the warts gradually disappeared.

J.A.J.

A favourite charm for warts, in the neighbourhood of Llansilin, was to go into the garden alone, when the beans were ripe, and take hold of the bean and rub the wart well, then bury it, at the same time taking care that no-one was looking on. This was said to be a certain cure.

January 25, 1905   *G.R.*

In some parts of North Wales, to my knowledge, credence was given to the following as ways of getting rid of warts:

a) Squeezing the sap from the stem of a dandelion, and rubbing the wart well with the sap;

b) Rubbing with fat bacon — it was believed this method would prove more effective if the bacon were buried and left to decay, by which time the wart would disappear;

c) Spitting on the wart the first thing directly a person awakes in the morning, the first spittle being considered a deadly poison.

February 8, 1905   *R.H.E.*

I was talking the other day to a medical man in Merionethshire, who has to go about a great deal among the agricultural folk, and who, talking Welsh, and a native of the county, is able to get at the true "innards" of things, when he said it was surprising what a hold superstition had still on the minds of the agricultural population, and how the old practises were still in vogue. He narrated a case within his own experience. A lady relative had a large wart on one of her fingers, and as she was an accomplished pianist the wart was not only a disfigurement to her dainty hand, but somewhat interfered with her playing. He tried to cure the wart by treating it with ethylate of sodium, which, as is well known, is about the strongest alkali a medical man can use. Nevertheless, the wart survived. The lady was then told to try the following remedy:

She had to get a turnip and cut off the top of it when the moon was full. She had then to scoop out a hole in the turnip, fill it with salt, and, replacing the top, put the turnip in a place where the moonbeams would fall on it. That being done, the wart was to be periodically anointed with the liquor found within the moonstruck turnip. She carried out the directions, and the wart duly disappeared. My friend did not tell me that the lady afterwards married the king's son and lived happily ever afterwards, but probably something of the kind happened.

October 1, 1902   *Meirion*

Hallowtide Customs

"It is customary in some parts of Wales (says a writer in the *Mirror* 1831) on 'All Hallow's E'en', or as it is styled by the sons of Gomer, 'Nos galan gauaf', for the superstitious country people to go to a certain window of the church, for the purpose, as it is said, of hearing a 'rara avis', yclept a ghost (with gravity be it spoken) pronounce sentence of death on all those who are doomed to go to their long homes during the year; and in some village churches, I am told that there are steps still extant, which are said to have been built purposely for the credulous to go up to the window to listen.

"The less credulous commemorate this eve by apple biting, nut cracking (as the English do on St Clement), and burning nuts, to ascertain who shall die that year; but the chef d'oeuvre is, they have a vessel styled the puzzling jug. From the brim, extending about an inch from the surface, it has holes fantastically made, so as to appear like ornamental work, and is not perceived but with much scrutiny. Three round nobs of the size of marbles are around the brim, having a hole of about the size of a small pea in each; the nobs communicate to the bottom of the jug, through the handle, which is hollow, and has a small hole at the top, which with two of the other holes, being stopped by the fingers, and mouth applied to the one nearest the handle, enables you to draw, or suck the contents with ease; but this trick is not known by every fool, and consequently, a stranger generally applies his mouth to the wrong place, and the contents of the jug are received in his neck 'or waistcoat, to no small 'diversion' of the spectators."

May 13, 1885   *Verax*

I am informed by a native of Corwen (Mr Wm Owen, now of Dinas Mawddwy) that it was the custom at Corwen about thirty-five years ago for women and children to go from house to house on All Saint's Day (November 1) to collect cakes called "Solod". The custom was called "Hen Solod". The cake was generally made of barley-flour, without any addition of more appetising ingredients than salt and water; and it was about one inch thick and four inches in diameter. Souling, I am told, still prevails in Shropshire, where contributions are solicited by singing the following doggerel:

"Soul! Soul! for a soul-cake;
Pray, good mistress, for a soul-cake.
One for Peter, and one for Paul,
Three for them who made us all.
Soul! Soul! for an apple or two;
If you've got no apples, pears will do.
Up with your kettle, and down with your pan,
Give me a good big one, and I'll be gone.
Soul! Soul! for a soul-cake, etc.
An apple or pear, a plum or a cherry,
Is a very good thing to make us merry."

(*The Leisure Hour*, 1876, pg730)

The lines, I think, will throw some light on the Corwen custom; and I would suggest that "Solod" is a corruption of soul with the Welsh termination -od – Soul-od. Mr Owen does not know whether the custom still survives at Corwen. But he mentioned that apples, bread and cheese, or any other articles of diet, were given at the houses where cakes had not been prepared, or had been distributed. The supplicatory doggerel at Corwen was much shorter than the English one:

"Dydd da i chwi heddyw,
Welwch chwi'n dda ga' i dipyn bach o fwyd
cenedl y meirw?" Amen.

"Cenedl y meirw", they said; whatever that may mean. May it not be a corruption of "Dy'gwyl y Meirw?"

I may also mention that it was customary at Dinas Mawddwy forty years ago, if not later, for children to go about on All Saint's Day to collect bread and cheese, which custom they called "Bara' chawsa". They used to ask for it in the following form:

"Bara' chawsa, bara' chawsa,
Os ca' i beth, mi neidia;
Os na cha' i ddim, mi beidia."

But it does not appear that the Dinas Mawddwy boys were so vulgar as to make use of rude remarks, or to mark the doors with chalk, in case of refusal, as I am told their contemporaries at Corwen used to.

March 25, 1891 *Glyn Trefnant*

The custom of going from house to house on All Saints' Day, and begging for the good will of neighbours, still survives in the parishes of Llangwm, Llanfihangel GM, and Cerrigydrudion. It is confined now to children, and the gifts are mostly small coins and apples, and pieces of bread and butter. When one asks what he wants, the child will answer "Hel bwyd cenad y meirw". (Ask for food as messenger of the dead).

May 24, 1893 *R.*

It may be well to place on record the exact words now sung on All Hallows' Eve. The boys who sung, asked where they learnt the words, seemed to think it a curious question: the words had come to them, probably, among their earliest impressions —

"Wissal wassal, bread and possal,
Apple or pear, plum or a cherry,
Any good thing to make us merry.
The roads are very dirty,
My shoes are very thin,
I've got a little pocket
To put a penny in.
If you haven't got a penny,
A ha'penny will do,
If you haven't got a ha'penny
God bless you!
Sol cake! sol cake!
One for Peter, two for Paul,
Three for the man that made us all.!"

November 13, 1895 *W.O.*

The church at Darowen is dedicated to St Tudur, the son of Arwystl Gloff, and the festival is — or rather was — held on October 15. In years long gone by the custom known as "Curo Tudur" formed an important item in the programme of the day. It was usual, on the night of the festival, for the youths of the neighbourhood to congregate in the village, and select one of their number — generally the most unpopular and defenceless — to represent Tudur. He was then carried about by those who were appointed for the purpose, whilst he was beaten on the back with sticks by others.

The origin of the custom is unknown, but if I might offer a guess, I think it is not unlikely that it was intended to commemorate the rough treatment which Tudur himself had suffered at the hands of those whom he endeavoured to benefit by the preaching of the true faith. Whatever the origin of it might be, I was informed, in the year 1889, by a woman who was bred and born in the village, that she had heard her grandfather many times relating that he had witnessed the ceremony of "Curo Tudur" performed in front of the old public house at Darowen. I scarcely think, from what she said, that there is anyone now living who remembers this peculiar custom.

February 21, 1894   *C.A.*

Rough Justice

From *The Evening Advertiser*, London, Friday, July 24th, 1801: "At Shrewsbury Quarter Sessions Mary Davis was sentenced to be imprisoned one year, and kept to hard labour, for milking a cow that did not belong to her."

March 19, 1902   *T.R.H.*

There are several curious entries in the old minute book in the early years of the Oswestry Incorporation, especially those relating to the punishment of paupers. Take the following as specimens:

"Nov 9, 1795. The determination of the Directors upon Mr Gibbons' and Mr Edwards' observation last week are that Mr Cooper [the Steward] be directed by the Board to put a chain and a log upon Red Moll's leg as a mark of disgrace for her misconduct in running away from this House and returning again with child.

"Oct 3, 1796. Ann Rowlands of Sweeney Mountain being convicted of receiving bread from Elizabeth Ffrancis one of the paupers in the House she appeared before the Board and penalty was mitigated to 5s. to be distributed in Bread at Moreton Chapel, and payment of the Constables

fees. The above-named Elizabeth Francis having for her offence been confined in the Solitary room for a week, and having been fed with bread and water, is now discharged on her promise to behave well for the future.

"Dec 31, 1798. John Jones a pauper in the House being this day convicted of stealing a Iron Wedge, the property of the Directors, from the House, and selling the same to John Jones of Oswestry blacksmith. It is ordered that he receive twenty-five lashes on the bare back in the dinner hall immediately in the presence of two of the Directors and of the paupers in the House.

"Oct 28, 1799. Ordered that all the single woman who shall come into the House in a state of Pregnancy shall be dressed in a particular manner by way of distinction and for the purposes of showing a due sense of their improper conduct, and that for the same purpose such women shall eat their meals at a separate table and shall be prevented as much as possible from mixing with the other inhabitants of the House; and Mr Cooper is ordered to prepare a dress for the inspection of the Directors at the next meeting."

January 12, 1876 *Jarco*

The following appears (p.62) in the report of the Historical Manuscripts Commission on the Shrewsbury Corporation Manuscripts:

"temp. Eliz. — Petition from Margaret Freman for release 'oute of this miserable prison' of the Burgess Gate, where she lies upon the bare boards, overpressed with irons, and ready to starve with hungers, justly punished for speaking certain idle words of Mr Tonks [Tomkys] the public preacher."

July 11, 1900   *W.O.*

The following petition, dated July 22, 1790, is from the Kenyon MSS at Gredington (Hist. MSS Commission): Petition to Lord Kenyon of Mrs Row and Mrs Bush, "two poor helpless women that has experienced a long and painful imprisonment of three years, by virtue of an *excommunicato capiendo* writ from the spiritual court, for being publickly married in the meeting house at Calverton, seven miles from Nottingham, in the same publick manner and form as quakers do." The pray that as they have never committed theft nor injured anyone, though they may perhaps be thought to have infringed some laws of man, that Lord Kenyon will look on them with an eye of pity, as Pharoah did to his chief butler, and restore them to their former station. What makes their infliction harder is that they and two small children have to sleep in one bed, and have to pay the jailer four shillings a week.

September 9, 1896   *Ed.*

The ancient Welsh custom, now nearly obsolete, known as riding the Ceffyl Pren — "Wooden Horse" — and intended to operate as a warning to faithless wives and husbands, was revived recently in an Anglesey village some three miles from Llangefni. The individual who had drawn upon himself the odium of his neighbours had parted from his wife.

On Saturday night, March 12, a large party surrounded his house, and, compelling him to get astride a ladder, carried him shoulder-high through the village, stopping at certain points to allow the womenkind to wreak their vengeance upon him. This amusement was kept up for some time, until the opportune arrival of a sergeant of police from Llangefni, who rescued the man. A number of summonses have been issued.

March 23, 1887   *Ed.*

"There is a custom in Shrewsbury (says Mr Hulbert, 'Hist. Co. Salop', 1835), and I believe in various parts of the county, and I have heard of its existence in some other counties, that when the illicit acquaintance of respectable persons become notorious or the meeting has been detected, a number of the lower orders assemble and make a Mawkin, that is stuff some old garments with straw, to resemble the suspected parties, which they carry through the streets, accompanying them with drumming on old drums and old cans, deafening shouts &c, always making a particular effort opposite the dwellings of the parties they intend to degrade."

Mr Hulbert goes on to say that serious consequences have at times arisen, and would have done so oftener, but that "judicious friends interfere, and with the bribe of a sovereign, a few cans of ale &c, prevail on the mob to disperse."

March 26, 1879   *Tell*

In a court case heard in the Divorce Division recently it was stated that straw had been tied around the gate of the petitioner's house in Monmouthshire. Counsel explained that in Monmouthshire it was a custom to tie straw in the front of a married couple's gate when the husband had been knocking his wife about, so that he might beat the straw instead of his wife.

May 24, 1893   *W.O.*

Some years ago it was customary in many Welsh villages to inflict the following punishment on persons guilty of swearing or disorderly conduct. The culprit was hoisted on the knees or the back of three or four of the company; all the rest uncovered, under a penalty; and then a person, who was usually chosen by lot, inflicted a series of blows with spade or shovel, reciting the following rhymes and at the same time dealing blows. The punishment was more effective than the services of half a score of policemen or ministers of religion!

"Fe dda'ru ti bechu a chwyddo dy foche,
A bwyta had mwstard, a diogi, ac eiste,
Os na faddeuir dy hen gamwedde,
Dy hen fontin di geiff ddiodde;
Whipping di hers cofia dy wers,
Twenty quavers cofia.
Bobyn y Gwyddel, un isel ei wal
A gadd ei wadd i'w ginio
Beth oedd yno iddo gael
Ond penwig wedi eu pwnio
"God Save the Queen"
Gŵr ar ei draed a gwaed ar ei fin — Chwibana."

The sufferer had to whistle as cheerily as he could, to show his gratitude to his tormentors, before he was allowed to go.

Another punishment was to "throw the culprit into hell." If he swore or used obscene words against those who had punished him he was tied or held on the ground, or in a hole, and then lifted up by his ears and his hair by Beelzebub (a name given to the one who administered the punishment) as many times as those present thought he deserved, all present helping to lift him up by his ears and his hair.

October 31, 1901   *J.L.W.*

Rolling Stoat

I read with much interest in your last issue a letter from Mr H. E. Forrest describing the condition of a stoat sent to Mr G. Cooke of Shrewsbury for preservation. Mr Forrest describes the stoat as entirely without fore legs, and asks how the animal so bereft could move about, and makes one or two suggestions as to the style of locomotion adopted. I think the following incident (the truth of which I will vouch for) may throw a little light on the matter.

A woodman employed on a large estate in South Oxen once told me that on the previous day he had seen a stoat robbing a pheasant's nest, and carrying the eggs to a wood stack a short distance off. The means adopted were as follows: The stoat first clasped an egg with his fore paws against his chest, resting his head upon them, and then rolling himself up into a complete ball with impetus from the hind legs rolled over and over until he reached the store-house. If a stoat with his full complement of legs could carry a pheasant's egg, I think he could manage personal locomotion when short of two. The woodman broke up the wood stack and found eighteen pheasant eggs stowed away.

October 12, 1904   *W. H. Bickerton*

Hedgehog Weapon

A few years ago a clergyman friend told me an anecdote about a Hedgehog, which I may here relate. A gentleman in the neighbourhood of Maidstone was going through one of his fields and found a large Hedgehog, which he thought would interest his people at home. He had put it in his handkerchief, as he had no other means of carrying it, and threw it over his shoulder. On getting to the road he was accosted by a tramp who demanded money in a threatening manner. Before the tramp could realise his danger, the gentleman hit him full in the face with the Hedgehog in the handkerchief.

The tramp with a howl, took to his heels, and the gentleman went and warned all the doctors and chemists in Maidstone to hand over to the police any man who might call to have his face dressed. The man did call at a doctor's place and was promptly handed over to the police punished for attempted highway robbery.

September 20, 1905   *Thos. Ruddy*

Strange Lights From The Sea

Seventy-five years ago, I find the district of Barmouth famous for unusual lights, and that much superstition then existed among the Cromlechs, as it still seems to exist, notwithstanding three-quarters of a century of science and education. In the *Mirror* of 28th Aug., 1830, appears the following:

"DEATH TOKENS IN WALES

In a wild and retired district in North Wales, that namely which extends westwards from Dolgelly to Barmouth and Towyn, where there is certainly as much superstition as there is in any other district of the same extent, and where there are many individuals who lay claim to the title and capabilities of seers, the following occurrence took place, to the great astonishment of the mountaineers. We can vouch for the truth of the statement, as many members of our own teulu, or class, were witness of the fact.

"One dark evening, a few winters ago, some persons with whom we are well acquainted, were returning to Barmouth on the south or opposite side of the river; as they approached the ferry-house at Penthryn, which is directly opposite Barmouth, they observed a light near the house, which they conjectured to be produced by a bon-fire, and greatly puzzled they were to discover the reason why it should have been lighted. As they came nearer, however, it vanished, and when they inquired at the house respecting it, they were surprised that not only had the people there displayed no light, but they had not even seen one, nor could they perceive any signs of it on the sands. On reaching Barmouth, the circumstances were mentioned, and the fact corroborated by some people there, who had also plainly and distinctly seen the light. It was settled, therefore, by some of the old fishermen, that this was a 'death-token', and, sure enough the man who kept the ferry at the time was drowned at high-water a few nights afterwards, in the very spot where the light was seen. He was landing from the boat, when he fell into the water, and so perished.

"The same winter the Barmouth people as well as the inhabitants of the opposite banks, were struck by the appearance of a number of small lights, which were seen dancing in the air. At a place called Borthwyn, about half a mile from the town, a great number of people came out to see these lights; and after a while they all but one disappeared, and this one proceeded slowly towards the water's edge, to a little bay where some boats were moored. The men in a sloop, which was anchored near, saw the light advancing — they also saw it hover for a few seconds over one particular boat, and then totally disappear. Two or three days afterwards the man to whom that particular boat belonged was drowned in the river while he was sailing about Barmouth in that very boat. We have narrated these facts just as they have occurred; we must leave the solution of the mystery to the ingenuity of our readers."

March 8, 1905   *K.G.S.*

Mr G. T. Picton-Jones, Yoke House, Pwllheli, writes in the *Field* as follows:

"Some years ago we witnessed here what we have never seen before — certain lights, eight in number, extending over, I should say, a distance of 8 miles; all seemed to keep their own ground, although moving in horizontal, perpendicular and zig-zag directions. Sometimes they were of a light blue colour, then like the bright light of a carriage lamp, then almost like an electric light, and going out altogether, in a few minutes would appear again dimly, and come up as before. One of my keepers, who is nearly 70 years of age, has not, nor has anyone else in this vicinity, seen the same before. Can any of your numerous readers inform me whether they are willo-the-wisps, or what? We have seen three at a time afterwards on four or five occasions."

February 24, 1875   *Ed.*

"Mr Picton-Jones has been kind enough to address to us the following letter, in response to the request which we made last week for further information:

'Yoke House, Pwllheli, 2nd March 1875 — The curious lights appeared again on Sunday night. We saw twelve at the same time, two were very bright, the one of a red, the other of a blue colour. They were inland, the same as before, but from what we could observe they did not confine themselves to marshy ground, although at first they seemed to rise from ground where we know there were swamps. It was a very dark and foggy night, and my brother, my son Percy, my keeper and I went out about a mile to see if we could get near them.

'When we had gone about half a mile, we observed four or five behind us. We went to the farm adjoining and called their attention to them. Mrs Picton-Jones and two servants watched them for an hour-and-a-half, and had from their description a better view than we had, as we were occasionally in hollows.

'On our way home from Bryntani Farm we saw a bright light at Yoke House, which we all thought was a lamp put out to direct us home, the night being so dark and our course across country. The other servants, by this time, having come home from church and chapel, were watching the curious antics of the lights. I should mention that we had a lamp with us, but it was darkened, except when we came to banks or ditches. Those at Yoke House saw the same light, and thought it was our lamp, but were all mistaken; as when we got within about 200 yards of our pond the light turned into a deep blue colour and disappeared.

'In front of the other pool there are some sheds, and one light that had appeared before we started seemed to go in, and out, round the corner, on to the cart horse stable, round its gable end, then on to the barn, exactly the same, as if it were a human being, with the exception of rising to such a height that even "Tall Agrippa" could not come up to it. Their movements and the distance over which they spread were the same as described before. Our house is about three quarters of a mile from the Cardigan Bay, and the promontory is about seven miles across as the crow flies. Last night they didn't appear, but we saw several flashes of lightning.

'I am sir, your obedient servant, G. T. Picton-Jones.' "

Cambrian News
Ed.

March 17, 1875

Having read the account by Mr Picton-Jones of the strange lights seen by him near Pwllheli, I beg to say that I witnessed a very similar phenomenon on the marshy ground near Borth. Some five or six years ago, owing to an accident on the Cambrian Railway, I had to post from Machynlleth to the neighbourhood of Towyn, where I was then residing. It would be about twelve o'clock pm, when I came in sight of the low ground and sandy dunes between Borth and the Dovey, the night being perfectly clear and still, and the stars shining, when to my astonishment I saw four or five lights moving apparently on the sandhills near the farm of Ynyslas.

I called the post boy's attention to them and never did I see a man so paralysed with fright; I thought that he would have fallen off the box, and the perspiration as I could see by the light of the lamps fairly ran down his face. He evidently considered them of supernatural origin as he told me an incoherent story of a boat's crew of shipwrecked foreigners having been murdered when they came ashore there many years ago (upon further enquiry, I find there was some tradition of the sort). However, there the lights were, moving about in a sort of aimless way until, as near as I can remember, we reached within a mile or two of Aberdovey. They were white, and about the size and brilliancy of the lamps carried by railway guards and porters.   •

March 24, 1875   *R.D.*

From time to time the West Coast of Wales seems to have been the scene of mysterious lights. In the 15th century, and again on a larger scale in the 16th, considerable alarm was created by fires that "rose out of the sea". Writing in January, 1694, the rector of Dolgelley stated that sixteen ricks of hay and two barns had been burned by "a kindled exhalation which was often seen to come from the sea."

In March, 1875, a letter by the late Mr Picton-Jones appeared in *Bye-gones* giving an account of curious lights which he had witnessed at Pwllheli; and now we have a statement from Towyn that within the last few weeks "lights of various colours have frequently been seen moving over the estuary of the Dysynni river and out at sea. They are generally in a northern direction, but sometimes they hug the shore and move at a high velocity for miles towards Aberdovey, and suddenly disappear."

October 13, 1877   *Ed.*

In a book entitled 'The Antiquities of England and Wales' by Francis Grosse, Esq., F.A.S., and published in 1787, there is the following curious allusion to the county of Merioneth:

"The county is very mountainous and unwholesome. The soil is rocky, reckoned the worst in Wales; yet produces some corn, sheep, deer, goats, fowls, game, and both fresh water and sea fish, particularly guiniad, salmon, trout, and herrings. It is subject to a livid fire or vapour that has destroyed everything in its course, except its inhabitants, which made great devestation in 1542 and 1564."

March 24, 1875 *Mary Edwards, of Dolserau*

In a sermon published in 1756 by the Rev Thomas Alcock of Plymouth, relating to the earthquakes at Lisbon, there is a note on p24 about the Harlech exhalations. It states that "at Harleck in Merioneth-shire about once a week, for many months together, in the night Time, there hovered about the Surface of the Earth, a luminous fiery Vapour of so destructive and deleterious a Nature that besides fireing a great many Hay Ricks, it poisoned the Grass wherever it came in such Manner that all the horses, cows, sheep, goats, hogs &c that eat of it immediately died."

March 8, 1882 *J.P.E.*

In 'Britania Depicta, or Ogilby Improved' (1720), under a map of Harlech and the district, are the following lines that may be of interest in view of the discussion now going on with regard to similar lights that are seen on the Welsh coast:

"'Tis credibly reported that in the year 1692 a Fiery Exhalation was seen to Cross the Sea, & to set Fire to the Ricks of Hay, Corn & Barns near Harlech & to infect the Grass, but it was not mischievous to Men though they were in the midst of it. It proceeded in the Night from the same Place for some Months, commonly on Saturdays or Sundays. The only Remedy to extinguish or drive it away was to sound Horns, Trumpets, or discharge Guns."

March 1, 1905 *T.R.H.*

(Although the date does not exactly agree, this refers no doubt, to the appearances described in the 'Philosophical Transactions' in 1694. - Ed.)

The following may be of special interest in connection with recent tales of mysterious lights in Wales:

1694, Apr 22. "A fiery exhalation rising out of the sea opened itself in Montgomeryshire a furlong broad and many miles in length, burning all straw, hay, thatch, and grass, hut doing no harm to trees, timber or any solid things, only firing barns or thatched houses. It left such a taint on the grasse as to kill all the cattle that eate of it. I saw the attestations in the hands of the sufferers. It lasted many months."

From 'Memoirs of Evelyn' (1819 Edition). Also in the *Montgomeryshire Collections*, for 1883.

July 12, 1905   *F.G.*

Mr G. T. Ryves, F.R.Met.Soc., in the *Daily News* of Saturday, writing from Llanfairfechan, calls attention to the unusually brilliant phosphorescence of the sea which had been visible there, and presumably at other seaside places, for some time past.

One night last week the display was exceptionally brilliant, and such as he had supposed was only seen in tropical or semi-tropical waters. A N.E. breeze, which sprung up about nightfall, produced a ripple upon the water, which had been quite smooth for several days, and as each wavelet broke upon the shingle, it emitted a flash of almost startling vividness, while along the whole shore there was a fringe, a yard or so in breadth, in which the waters flowered with a less brilliant, but unmistakenly phosphorescent light, and far out in the bay one could distinctly see the crests of the incoming waves shining with the same phosphorescent glow.

A handful of shingle thrown into the water produced an effect which he could only compare to the "jewelled bouquet" in pyrotechnic displays, and he was told by those who were rowing after dark that the flash of light caused by each stroke of the oar was even more remarkable than that produced by the breaking of the sea upon the shore. The colour of the light was of a bluish hue, not unlike that from the electric arc-light.

August 28, 1895   *Ed.*

Undying Love

The following extract is copied from a book entitled 'The Anecdote Library', lent me some years ago by Mr W. S. Buddicom of Ticklerton Hall. The book had apparently been rebound and was incomplete as regards date of publication, which I imagine to be the early part of the 19th century:

"Sir John Pryce of Newtown, Montgomeryshire, married three wives, and kept the first two who died in his room, one on each side of his bed; his third lady, however, declined the honour of his hand till the defunct rivals were committed to their proper place. During the season of miracles worked in 1748 by Bridget Bostock of Cheshire, who treated all diseases by prayer, faith and an embrocation of fasting spittle, multitudes resorted to her from all parts, Sir John wrote the following letter to this wonderful woman, to make him a visit at Newtown Hall, in order to restore to him his third and favourite wife, now dead:

" 'Madam — Having received information by repeated advices, both public and private, that you have, of late, performed many wonderful cures even when the best physicians have failed, and that the means used appear very inadequate for the effects produced, I cannot but look upon you as an extraordinary and highly favoured person; and why not may the same merciful God, who enables you to restore sight to the blind, hearing to the deaf, and strength to the lame, also enable you to raise the dead to life? Now, having lately lost a wife, whom I most tenderly loved, my children an excellent step-mother, and our acquaintances a very dear and valuable friend, you will lay us all under the highest obligations, and I earnestly entreat you, for God Almighty's sake, that you will put up your petitions to the Throne of Grace on our behalf, that the deceased may be restored to us, and the late dame Eleanor Pryse be raised from the dead. If your personal attendance appears to you to be necessary, I will send my coach and six, with proper servants, to wait on you hither, whenever you please to appoint. Recompense of any kind, that you could propose, would be made with the utmost gratitude; but I wish the bare mention of it is not offensive to both God and you.

'I am, Madam, your obedient &c.,

John Pryse.' "

April 11, 1900   *T. Caswell*

True Survivors

A few days before Christmas I found a primrose in bloom in my garden. I placed a flower pot over it to preserve it, intending to gather it in a day or two. The snow came and covered the pot over for eight weeks, and when the pot was lifted three primroses in bloom were to be seen.

March 13th, 1895   *Ed.*

I was with my brother-in-law on the 28th of August, 1895, when he got a small plant of the common maidenhair fern (*Asplenium Trichomanes*) from a wall on the side of the river Conway near Bettws-y-Coed. He wrapped it up in a piece of paper and intended to put it in his fern case on his return to London. It remained in his pocket quite forgotten until the middle of June of this year. Strange to say it seemed to have some life in it, and was at once planted in the fern case where it soon began to send up fresh fronds, and at present (end of August) it is in a flourishing healthy state.

September 9, 1896   *Thos. Ruddy*

In the Add. MS., 14, 974 fol. 74, at the British Museum, there is a fragment, without any heading or signature, of a letter, which gives an account of a long-lived cat at Nantglyn, in Denbighshire. The writer states that he had just received a communication, by post, from Neuadd Wen, on the afternoon of July 6th, 1728, to the effect that there was a cat at Nantglyn, near Denbigh, which was 140 years of age. Several people remembered it for more than sixty years. Mr William Lloyd of Pennant, its owner, remembered it for fifty-eight years; and he gives an account of the cat, and his own family as well, wherein he states that his grandmother, who was born in the 35th year of the reign of Elizabeth (1593), had reared this cat, and had it since she was five years of age.

Of course it does not matter much when the poor cat was born; but if we compare the dates, it was born in 1598, when Mr Lloyd's grandmother was 5 years of age. Therefore it could not be more than 130 in the year 1728.

December 11, 1895   *C.A.*

Writing upon 'Fasting' in the *St James's Gazette* many years ago, Dr Forbes Winslow observes: "In 1770 a woman living at Barmouth created considerable excitement and amazement in the world. She was reported to have lived for seven years and a half without tasting food, her lips only moistened with water."

August 23, 1893   *B.*

"They write from Denbigh, in Wales, that a young woman hanged there for child murder, recovered as they were carrying her to be buried, and put her hand out of the coffin; the hangman attempted to carry her back to the place of execution to hang her again; but the mob fell upon him and knocked out his brains, and rescued the woman." (From the *Postman* for October 11th, 1701).

April 16, 1905   *W.O.*

What's In A Name?

"What is most impressive in Debrett's record of the Rev W. L. Tollemache-Tollemache is the extraordinary space occupied by the name of his children. They are ten in number and they have ninety Christian names among them. No wonder the humble farmers of South Wytham dare not approach the front of the Rectory lest they should happen to meet Master Lyulph Ydwallo Odin Nestor Egbert Lyonel Toedmag Hugh Erchenwyne Saxon Esa Cromwell Orma Nevill Dysart Plantagenet Tollemache-Tollemache, aged eight; or Miss Lyona Decima Veronica Esyth Undine Cyssa Hylda Rowena Adela Thyra Ursula Ysabel Blanche Lelias Dysart Plantagenet Tollemache-Tollemache, aged six." (*Mark Lane Express*).

October 15, 1884   *Ed.*

Chance In A Million

The following startling and authentic coincidence is vouched for by trustworthy local authorities. On December 5th, 1664, a boat crossing the Menai Strait with eighty-one passengers on board encountered a terrific gale, and foundered. The only man who escaped death was a Mr Hugh Williams. More than a hundred years later, on December 5th, 1780, another vessel with a large number of passengers were drowned except one, again a Mr Hugh Williams. Again, on December 5th, 1820, a boat laden with thirty people sank in the same spot. The sole survivor once more was a Mr Hugh Williams.

February 14, 1900   *Ed.*

The Rev David Lloyd of Crewkerne, Somerset, at one time curate of Llangollen, writes to the *Strand Magazine* for February: "Urged by a large number of my friends, I write to bring to your notice a unique and very remarkable coincidence that happened in my family. We have three children, and they were born as follows — Myfanwy, our eldest, on January 21st, 1900; Nesta, on January 21st, 1901; Robert, on January 21st 1902. Not only were they born on the same day but also the very same hour, viz. 2 am."

February 18, 1903   *Ed.*

The following extract is taken from Dr Burney's 'Collection of Newspapers in the British Museum (vol CXVI): The London Post, with Intelligence Foreign and Domestic, Aug 19-21, 1700:' "We have advice from Staffordshire that one Pendrell (being the last of the family* that was instrumental in saving King Charles II by hiding him in the oak, ever after called the Royal Oak, after the battle of Worcester) has departed this life; but that which makes his death very remarkable is that the very day and hour that he died the said oak was blown down by a storm in the wind."
*ie the last survivor of those who personally assisted in the king's escape, not the last survivor of the Pendrell family.
February 8, 1899   *L.C.O.*

The following cutting from *Aris's Birmingham Gazette* of May 16, 1796, may be of some interest to the readers of BYE-GONES: "The following instances of the precarious tenure by which we hold this mortal life lately occurred at Llanarmon, near Oswestry — The Rev Mr Williams, vicar of the parish, died very suddenly, and his brother, the curate of Llanfillin, having been sent for on the occasion, dropped down dead soon after entering the house. The widow also of the deceased vicar expired last week, after a very few hour's illness."
June 10, 1896   *W. Holloway Bott*

From *The Albion*, July 20th, 1801: "Some months since a boy fatigued with playing got into an old boat that was drawn up on the beach at Borth Ferry, near Bangor, and fell asleep. The tide was higher than usual, and floated the boat away, so that when the child awoke he found himself at sea beyond the view of land. In this perilous situation he remained for thirty hours, when he was picked up by a Liverpool trader and carried to Dublin. He returned home some weeks since, and a few days afterwards, playing near a small pool at Oakland Carding Manufactory, Llanrwst, he fell in, and was drowned."
March 19, 1902   *Ed.*

An Insult To The English

"Cyn codi cŵn Caer" is an old Welsh adage, which is often used in North Wales. There was a very strong feeling of animosity between the Kymru and the English before the time of Edward the First, and for many years afterwards, until Henry VII slackened the yoke which pressed so heavily on his countrymen. The feeling was so intense on the side of the Welsh that they never used to call their neighbours men, but always dogs.

The Welsh on their part used to look for every opportunity to rush on the English border towns for the sake of pillage, especially Chester, which was the chief English stronghold on the borders. The English erected a large fortress near Chester bridge, and set sentinels there to watch the town during the night. Every time the Welsh intended to make an attack on the old city, these dogs, as they were called, were always awake. Thus at last it became a proverb in Wales that if a Cymro should happen to see a neighbour about earlier than usual in the morning he would say "So-and-so is up before Chester dogs."

April 11, 1883 (*From 'Cymru Fu' — Ed.*)

An Insult To The Welsh

Andrew Borde, in his 'Boke of Knowledge', written in the 16th century, characterizes the Welsh thus:

"I am a Welshman, and do dwel in Wales,
I have loved to serche budgets and to look in males;
I love not to labour, nor to delve nor to dyg,
My fingers be lymed lyke a lyme twyg;
And whereby riches (come) I do not greatly set,
Syth all is fysshe that cometh to the net."

January 7, 1874 *Eliola*

The Historian's Revenge

The following is preserved in the British Museum Library —
Hynod Beth

Mr Ll-d of H-f-d-n-s being among the antiquarians who out of curiosity opened the tomb of King Edward I at Westminster Abbey on May 2, 1774, as soon as the body appeared he spat in his face calling him the vilest tyrant that ever was a curse to mankind for his cruelty in slaughtering the innocent Welsh Bards, and added that 'if he could have done it with decency he would have p-ss-d on him'. This act of revenge upon the dead

116

monarch was told to his present Majesty, King George III, who seemed well pleased with the farce."

April 8, 1882   *Nemo*

The Future

"I am going to vacuum the dining room," said one of the inmates of my house, a native of Wales, the other day. Though there is no special connection with the BYE-GONES district in this Note, since it was the first time I had heard "vacuum" used in this way, it may be interesting to record here a usage which will, doubtless, become general now that vacuum cleaners have been introduced.

January 21, 1914   *O.*

On Friday the Motor Car Act of 1903 comes into force. By it owners of motor cars and motor cycles will have to register their car or cycle with the County Council and get from the same authority a licence to drive, which has to be renewed annually. Each car and motor cycle must carry a plate bearing the index mark of the Council with whom the motor is registered, and the separate number assigned the driver by the Council. In Shropshire the index letters are "A.W."; for Montgomeryshire "E.P."; for Denbighshire "C.A."; and for Merionethshire "F.F." Up to yesterday 54 motor cars and 24 motor cycles had been registered with the Salop County Council.

A great deal of trouble arose with regard to the number 13. In the ordinary course of these applications this fateful numeral in the list of cars fell to the lot of a lady motorist. She, however, promptly, had it sent back, and without any hint of some strangely overpowering superstition about the number, said she would prefer a change. Needless to say, the change was acceded to, and the lady's motor car now has less ominous figures than "13". This, however, was not the end of the difficulty. A chauffeur sent to register his master's car accepted No.13 without moving a hair. That chauffeur, however, came back next day with the message that his master's daughter would be better satisfied with another number!

"Thirteen" after this was not tried again with cars, and is now cancelled so far as Salop is concerned. In motor cycles this "unlucky number" was accepted by an owner who is a farmer, and despite all the folk-lore of the rural districts, has not yet returned to make a change.

December 30, 1903   *Ed.*

Some day, perhaps, "Jack the Ripper" will be one of the puzzles of the antiquary. So far has it already entered into popular speech, *horibile dictu*, that even children are heard to use it in anger, or, stranger still, in accents of persuasion, in their play in the streets. Two or three days ago a small child in Oswestry streets was heard saying to another who was in distress "Never mind, you shall be Jack the Ripper." It seems worth while to put on record that the name was given in this year, 1888, to a wretch who committed a number of horrible and undiscovered crimes of murder and mutilation in the East End of London.

December 26, 1888   *W.O.*

BYE-GONES — Holders of the earlier volumes are fortunate in possessing books that have been "out of print" for a considerable period, and are now much enhanced in money value. A copy was recently sold at a book auction in London for 22s that had cost its owner 7s 6d. And, as only a very limited number are printed, the later volumes are fast becoming scarce.

May 11, 1881   *Ed.*